Christi

M000120107

'Best Parenting Book'

Recommended by:

Josh D. McDowell

Author & Speaker

"...I encourage you to read this book because it will touch you, minister to you and my hope is that you will conclude, as I did, that you will become a better person and parent as the result of reading, *Growing Up With Jessica*."

Award Winning Author
James Walker
One of three WINNERS for
'Grand Prize Overall'
Christian Choice Book Awards.

Pastor Rick Warren
Saddleback Church

"When God gives us a challenge, He also gives us the strength and wisdom to complete it. Sharing your heart and your experiences... is a great testimony of God's faithfulness... It's obvious that God is using... your family in a great way. Give Jessica a hug for me."

1

What Our Readers are saying...

"...I know I won't be able to find the proper words to describe how I felt while reading it and when I was finished. What best describes what I am thinking and feeling is the statement: 'My heart is full.' "

"...this is an excellent book... I am so glad you shared your story. It was heartfelt and I admire your courage, faith and love of Jessica. God bless you."

"...this was the best discussion our book club has ever had... what a great experience for all of us..."

"...everyone loved the *'dream chapter'* and thought it was extremely powerful... also the paragraph about Jessica in heaven was such a beautiful picture."

...I feel closer to God in ways that I can't find the words to express. Thank you. You did a wonderful job of sharing your story... "

"...Once I started, I could not put it down until I finished. It is a powerful book. One everyone should read."

"...it is my prayer that this book will... touch a million more people the way it has touched me..."

"...the unconditional love for children parallels God's love for us..."

Growing Up

with
JESSICA

*Blessed by the Unexpected Parenting
of a Special Needs Child.*

Tenth Anniversary Edition

Second Edition 2009-15
Updated & Revised 2015

Growing Up with JESSICA: A True Story.
Blessed by the Unexpected Parenting
of a Special Needs Child.

by James Walker

Printed in the United States of America

Print-ISBN: 978-0-9800641-0-0
eBook-ISBN: 9780980064124

Unless otherwise indicated all Bible quotations are taken from the NIV
©1988,1989,1990,1991 by Tyndale House Publishers and the
NCV © 2003 by Thomas Nelson, Inc.

www.greatnewspress.com
FAM033000-Family & Relationships: Children with Special Needs
FAM012000-Family & Relationships: Parent & Adult Child
FAM028000-Family & Relationships: Learning Disabilities

Growing Up with JESSICA

Dedication

This book is dedicated with love to
Jessica's big brother Jon and big sister Jamie.
Without their love, support and unselfishness
I couldn't have told this story.

Also, to my wife Renée,
who in my mind, is exactly the Mother
she always wanted to be.

Growing Up with JESSICA

Jim, Jessica's father, approached me when I was in Boise to do a series of meetings. It is my normal practice to go into the auditorium before my seminars to chat and meet those in attendance. It was during this time that Jim introduced himself and showed me his book. It was in a binder with the picture of a sweet young girl in a red dress on the cover. The title was *'Growing Up With Jessica.'*

The book immediately caught my attention as he explained who Jessica was and what his family had been dealing with for about 25 years. I asked if he had a copy that I could take with me to read and he smiled and handed me the binder with the complete manuscript inside. I gave him my contact information and he agreed to call me in about three weeks.

In the weeks and months ahead, I read the book and passed it on to my wife, Dottie, my daughter, Kelly, and others as well. We were touched by the story. Dottie said to me, *"Josh, every parent in America should read this book!"* Dottie's comment impressed me since she has a very good and critical eye for such things. She can be hard to impress and yet she *"...loved it!"* I decided to meet with Jim the next time I was in Boise to relay our impressions back to him. I wondered what his plans were in regard to getting the book published.

The return trip to Boise was a whirlwind of activities, but I did get to meet and talk with Jim. I shared the thoughts of my family and then posed the question, *"Jim, what are you going to do with this book?"*

He looked at me, shrugged his shoulders, and said, *"I don't know Josh. I really don't know where this is going. I wrote the book in the hopes of helping others who may be facing adversity. I thought that sharing our story would be an encouragement to them, both now and in the future."*

Since that day, I have been encouraging Jim to get his story in print.

After reading the final manuscript, I asked for three copies. I shared them with others and the response was always the same, *"...an excellent book!"*

When I first saw *'Growing Up With Jessica'* I thought maybe it was something for 'special needs' families, and there is no doubt that there is a great need for that category of book out there. But then we realized that this book was not confined to any single group. Literally, anyone, but especially parents, could relate to and benefit from this book and the information contained in it.

It was truly a joy to learn that Jim had taken the steps to get this book in print, because it meets readers' needs on many different levels. I was very happy to contribute the forward to this book.

Whether you are a believer or not, young or old, parent or not, I encourage you to read this book because it will touch you, minister to you and my hope is that you will conclude, as I did, that you will become a better person and parent as the result of reading *'Growing Up With Jessica.'*

Josh D. McDowell
Author and Speaker

Notes from Jessica's Dad.

This is a true story which I have shared
as clearly and accurately as possible.
I have used both my recollections and notes and letters
as well as the recollections and notes of others
written and preserved over the years.

In addition, I have used the copies of Jessica's medical records,
including physicians notes, now in my possession.

Some of the actual names have been changed or omitted,
to respect and protect the privacy of others, who were
involved in Jessica's life, and this retelling of it.

And finally, a thank you to everyone for their support
and encouragement with this project.

It is my sincere hope that you will receive
as big a blessing from reading this story
as we have... as we lived it.

Growing Up with JESSICA

A Tiny Heartbeat...

1965

...the Seed of Love is Planted.

Growing Up with JESSICA

Chapter 1

A tiny heartbeat... the seed of love is planted.

I strained to listen.

I held my breath.

I was listening for a miracle... a miniature miracle. Suddenly, as the doctor moved the sensor slightly on my wife Renée's abdomen... there it was... my first contact with our unborn child... a persistent swishing sound... a tiny heartbeat.

I was in love again.

Renée and I had met when we were both seniors in high school. We met one night at a pizza parlor and that summer after our graduation we fell deeply in love. It was the first time I had really been in love... real love. We dated for about three years and were married on January 15, 1965.

Renée came from a broken home where her mother had deserted her and her brother. She had a very strained relationship with her mother as she was growing up and she was deeply hurt by her childhood experiences. She and her brother Ron were raised by her single father who was 44 years old when Renée, the youngest, was born.

Although neither of us had a solid Christian background, we began our life together, even before we were married, committed to finding some answers to life and everlasting love. Renée did not want her marriage to end in failure, neither did she want her children to experience the pain and heartbreak she had known. We wanted a life together that would last. It was at this time that we began visiting churches and looking for something solid we could count on for help with the storms of life, that would sooner or later surely come into our lives. Eventually, we turned to the only thing we both were at least vaguely familiar with... the Bible.

I remember at our wedding, we chose to get on our knees and recite the *Lord's Prayer* as a symbol of our commitment to seek the truth in our lives together.

After our marriage, we began a process of seeking answers to life's deeper questions. Questions like:

> *Was God really out there somewhere?*

> *Were the Bible's promises true?*

> *What was real true love all about?*

We sensed that something was missing in our lives-something we needed... but... what was it?

In our third year of marriage, our first child was born on June 20, 1968. After a long and difficult labor, which went well over 24 hours, a little girl came to begin our family. We named her Jamie Ann. Three years later, on July 14, 1971, we were all joined by her little brother Jon David.

We thought our family was complete. You know like the lyrics to a song "*... a girl for you... a boy for me... oh... my dear... how happy we will be...*" ,but the story didn't end there.

Renée and I had attended a '*Marriage Encounter*' program for enriching our marriage, in early December, 1977. Within a month or so, she had begun to experience what appeared to be morning sickness. We didn't want to face it, but was it possible she was pregnant? That's the way it looked, and so, we scheduled an appointment with the doctor to confirm our suspicions. The unexpected had happened.

The doctor cleared his throat and seemed embarrassed and uncomfortable, fidgeting on his stainless steel stool, and avoiding our gaze. We looked at him nervously wondering if something was wrong with that precious little heartbeat. I could still hear it echoing in my head, and my heart somehow felt warmer in the comfort of that... swish... swish... swishing sound. I could hear the sound of my own heart rising in my ears as we waited for him to continue.

"Of course due to your age, and the fact that you said this was not a planned pregnancy," the doctor mumbled, still avoiding any direct eye contact, *"...uhhh..... you could at this early stage... ummm... er... abort this fetus..."* He gulped for air, *"...you could easily terminate this pregnancy."* He finished with a profound blush as his shoulders sagged.

Thump! Thump! Thump! Went my heart. The silence in the room was deafening as Renée and I absorbed what he had just said. Finally at last our eyes met. I looked into her warm and tender brown eyes. It was like looking into the eyes of a doe who had just been confronted by a rifle shot. I could see the shock of the doctor's words, reverberating with horror, through her body and soul. She was pleading for help with her eyes. I shook my head slowly.

I remember that with one voice, and with our eyes locked on each other, we said with a conviction that came from somewhere deep inside, *"NOOO! NO, we DEFINITELY... WANT... THIS... BABY!"* A new life had begun between us and I think at that moment we both felt the fierceness of our love for the new little person we had created... this new seed of our love.

We had decided. This child was going to be born and grow and prosper in our family, and we would love this child forever.

We had at that time of course, no inkling of how much this unexpected child would ultimately alter and enrich us. We were about to be changed very deeply, and in so many ways. We could not even start to imagine.

So with that decision behind us, the growing slowly began.

Looking back now, I can see that the commitment we had made that day, was a decision that changed the course of our lives.

That one tiny heartbeat.

At Last We Meet...

1978

...Jessica the 'Blessed One'

Chapter 2

At last we meet... Jessica the 'blessed one.'

Step by step the woman inched toward the crevice in the earth, as if drawn closer by some irresistible force. Suddenly a pale hand reached up from the darkness and grabbed her ankle and she began to scream, *"...NOOOO!"*

"Mr. Walker... Mr. Jim Walker!" The gentle, but professional sounding voice of the maternity room nurse had interrupted my focus on the television in the waiting room.

"You have a beautiful baby girl, Mr. Walker," she gushed, with an excited smile. *"Would you like to come meet her?"*

It was August 25, 1978, my wife's 34th birthday. I was feeling a little unprepared, since this baby, our third child, was not expected for at least another three weeks.

Earlier that day, Renée had been at her brother's house, and as she was walking across the lawn, she stepped in a small hole and fell. She wasn't hurt, but her water had broken, and soon after her contractions started. After a quick call to the doctor we headed off to the maternity ward. There was no doubt, this little baby was coming to join us soon, and very soon, ready or not! This baby seemed to be full of surprises.

Everything went very smoothly at the hospital.

Later that night, I sat half asleep in a small stuffy waiting room, trying to keep myself awake by watching an old horror movie called, 'The Night of the Living Dead.' After a short search, the nurse had found me.

Rubbing my eyes, I walked into the half-darkened recovery room and the first thing I saw was Renée's beaming smile. She has a very radiant smile, a way of smiling with her entire heart and soul, and this time she was lighting up the room.

I looked beside her on the gurney and saw a beautiful little red faced girl with the biggest dimples. She had worked one arm free and was waving it in my direction as if to say 'come closer dad.' Instinctively I reached out for her hand and she instantly grabbed my finger with a fierce grip.

The watching nurses murmured in the background. "*Wow! Look at that grip. She sure knows her daddy!*"

At last I had met this mysterious little stranger and she was a stranger no more. Even though Renée and I, at that point, had not come up with a name for our new little girl, we had loved her deeply when we first heard her heartbeat, that fateful day in the doctor's office. So this is what little '*swish... swish*' looks like, I thought, as I studied her face carefully, it was hard to stop smiling.

Watching our first meeting, the nurse asked me if I would like to accompany her, to assist in weighing and placing my new little girl in the hospital nursery.

I felt so proud, as I helped roll her down the hall. Every time I reached out with my finger she would seize it with her tight little grip and hold on.

As we held her in the scale the nurse had looked at her long slender and rather delicate looking fingers. *"Oh! Look!"* she said with great enthusiasm, *"She has the hands of a pianist. She's going to grow up to be a great concert pianist!"* And I said, while smiling proudly with a father's pride, *"absolutely..."* and then again louder, *"...absolutely!"*

Even to this day, many years later, the images of that first meeting with our new baby girl, so full of promise and excitement, are fresh in my mind. I often replay the scene, slowly in my mind, and it always affects me.

I have discovered over the years at various times, that the events and images of that day sometimes encourage me, and other times taunt me with the bittersweet taste of unfulfilled dreams. However, they always inspire me to do my best to live up to the promise of that day... *'absolutely.'*

The next few days were a whirlwind of new born activity. Friends and relatives came to visit, admiring our new little one. Renée was beaming proudly, as our two other children, Jamie, age ten, and Jon, age seven, met her for the first time. It was a precious moment.

I remember going to the department store and finding Renée a beautiful new night gown and robe. Excitedly, I rushed down to the hospital on my lunch hour to surprise her with it.

To my disappointment, she was gone from her room. *"Having a bath,*" I was told and so I took the gown and robe out of the box and laid it out across her bed and then rushed back to work.

Later that afternoon, I got an excited call from Renée, "*The robe and nightgown are perfect!*" she said, "*I Love them! Thank you! I love you!*" I could feel her love coming through the phone. I didn't know it then... but her next phone call would be very different.

Early the next morning however, all was well, and '*baby Walker*' became '*Jessica Elizabeth Walker*'. Our baby had a name! We had chosen '*Jessica*' because it meant '*blessed one*'. Her middle name was chosen after my mother's middle name. We found out later that it meant '*consecrated to God*'.

My last name '*Walker*' comes from the root of '*forester*' or '*one who walks among the forest,*' and so our baby girl would be... '*Blessed one... consecrated to God... who walks among the forest...*' How could anyone not succeed with a name like that?

We had no idea at that time, how meaningful and comforting the deeper meaning of the names we had chosen so lightheartedly that day, would be to us, and to many others, as the years passed by.

Jessica '*the blessed one*' was here.

A Cloud of Doubt...

1978

...Tears Falling Like Rain.

Chapter 3

A cloud of doubt... tears falling like rain.

The phone in my office rang.

Pre-occupied with my work, I picked up the receiver and
mumbled *"Hello?"* no answer, *"HELLO!"* still no answer.
I started to hang up, but at the last instant, I heard something.
It sounded like a sobbing... a gasping and then more crying.
A bolt of emotion shot through my heart, *"Renée?"* no answer...
"Renée is that you?"

It was the morning of the day that Jessica would be coming home
from the hospital. I had gone in early that day to finish an urgent
project so that I could take off work that afternoon and spend
the rest of the day at home with Renée and Jamie and Jon and of
course Jessica. It would be our first evening together as an
'expanded' family. Jessica and her proud little mother were
coming home at last.

Everything was ready and waiting: a pretty little crib, sweet
little baby blankets and a slew of new toys of every description,
not to mention a breathlessly expectant, big brother and sister.

All things were now ready. Excitement was in the air, because
today was the big day!

"Jessica can't come home with me," my wife gasped between
sobs, *"...she has to stay in the hospital!"* she moaned, as her tears
fell like rain. I had never heard her so completely despondent.

She sounded heartbroken. My mind was whirling! Suddenly without warning, a cloud of doubt and uncertainty had cast a shadow across our happy lives.

Images of Jessica, backed up by Renée's sobbing, filled my mind. *'What was happening? What had gone wrong? Why had this come about?'*

I guess I responded in the same mind-numbed way many parents do when their child is in danger. I tried to compose myself. I fought back the sense of panic, as I tried to calmly speak to Renée. Our hearts were beating and hurting as one. I assured her over and over that everything would be okay, but as I hung up the phone, I felt crushed.

I got on the phone to our family doctor and then the insurance carrier. The problem was an elevated *'bilirubin level'* which is an infant form of *'jaundice'*. This was new to my vocabulary, but apparently often occurring in premature babies like Jessica.

After intense negotiations on the phone, inspired by the memory of Renée's sobbing ringing in my ears, I was able to reverse their decision.

If Jessica was staying in the hospital, then Renée would be staying as well. I relayed the information to Renée later that day and then headed off for the hospital to see her and Jessica.

We talked everything over and that helped to calm us both down for the time being. I tip-toed out after Renée fell into an exhausted sleep after nursing Jessica. A crisis had passed.

After two more days in the hospital, with periodic monitoring of *'bilirubin levels'* in her blood, little Jessica improved enough to go home with us on a conditional basis.

The condition she was released under was that every morning at 7:30 am as long as was medically needed, we would take her in for blood tests, as an outpatient.

So began the first week of Jessica's life at home. For eight days we would arise early and head down to the hospital. It was a new and unforgettable experience for all of us.

Facing the squirming and crying on a daily basis, as her tiny arms and legs were jabbed with needles to draw the necessary blood, was excruciating for us all, especially for Renée.

To say that it was traumatic to inflict such pain on an innocent such as our new baby girl would be an understatement, but it was necessary to help her, and so we steeled ourselves and toughed it out. We began to grow stronger.

Finally, to our profound relief, she was declared okay by the medical staff and the daily trauma was over. The calming effect of a more normal daily routine was welcomed. The big black clouds of doubt and uncertainty had receded and the falling tears seemed like a distant memory. Life was rosy again.

The kids were back in school, the weather had cooled and a beautiful *'Indian Summer'* was on the horizon. The kids and I picked apples off of the Golden Delicious Apple Tree in our back yard. I love to make things out of wood, and that summer I had built a small cider press, and so we squeezed some fresh cider and we all enjoyed it.

Jessica was back to being a normal baby and we were getting to know her better every day.

Late that night, I sat on the patio and listened to the crickets sing as I sipped my warm apple cider and pondered the three week wild ride we had just gone through. I was relieved to see everyone happy and healthy again.

On my way to bed, after I checked on Jamie and Jon, I stopped to look at Jessica sleeping peacefully in her crib, showing no ill effects, in spite of all she had been through.

'*Welcome home,*' I thought to myself.

At last, Jessica was safe at home and the crisis had passed like a bad dream... or so we thought at the time.

We had no idea what was coming.

An Unexpected Mystery Appears...

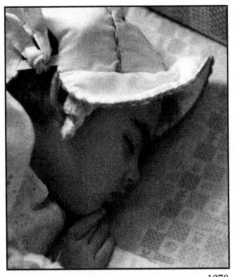

1978

...a Parent's Worst Nightmare.

Growing Up with JESSICA

Chapter 4

An unexpected mystery appears... a parent's worst nightmare.

I stood over Jessica's crib in the semi-darkness, silently watching her sleep, clutching my camera as I waited for the morning light to flood the room.

My normal daily routine is to be up early and I enjoyed watching her slow peaceful breathing. I know that beauty isn't the true measure of a child's worth, but she was a very beautiful child of two and a half months. She had her mother's eyes and olive complexion and for a small baby she had lots of shiny, jet black hair. She seemed just about perfect to me, as I gazed at her. A perfectly lovely little girl, and so angelic as she lay there.

Suddenly as she began to stir, she twitched and her head jerked to the left, then her body stiffened for just an instant and all was peaceful again. *"What was that?"* I wondered aloud. Probably nothing although, I did recall seeing other funny movements which were similar, perhaps not as hard, but the same general pattern, usually when she was waking up.

My thoughts turned to the events on Halloween night, just two weeks before. I had taken the kids *'trick or treating'* that night and Renée and Jessica had gone to church, since Renée had a choir practice.

Later that evening when we all got back together, I remember going out to the car to carry Jessica into the house, and the first thing Renée said to me, with a slight tremor in her voice was,

"Something is wrong with Jessica..." her voice trailed off in the dark, but I could see the look of alarm on her face. I looked at Jessica. She was sleeping like an angel, nothing seemed amiss.

"What do you mean? What's wrong?" I said, feeling puzzled.

Apparently, Jessica had cried all evening in the nursery, and although several of our friends tried to comfort her, she was unconsolable. Finally they came and got Renée. Eventually Jessica had gone to sleep in her arms and Renée came home.

It was puzzling, although Jessica had received her first DPT vaccination that morning and they said she might be fussy. That was probably it we decided, and that seemed like a reasonable explanation at that time.

The next day after that Halloween night, I had left early for work and so I didn't see Jessica at all until later that evening. It was my habit to play with her as soon as I got home. I would sit her on my knee hold her little hands and bounce her and make noises and she would watch me intently and coo back.

When I picked her up on that day she had seemed distant, almost like a stranger to me. It had been disturbing and I felt rather uncomfortable. Something had seemed very different.

As I stood over her crib, I couldn't help but wonder if there was a connection between what I was now seeing and that Halloween incident. I couldn't shake my uneasiness. I decided to ask Renée about it.

When I mentioned to Renée at breakfast, what I had seen, she confirmed that she had seen the jerky movements as well. I said nothing more about it, but I didn't feel very good about what I had seen and I was determined to pay closer attention in the future, to Jessica's not so random movements.

In the days ahead, Renée and I became increasingly convinced that something mysterious was happening to Jessica. Renée had mentioned it to our family doctor in a phone call, but he had not been concerned. *"Babies do all kinds of funny things..."* he calmly reassured her. As the weeks passed, the strange pattern became more and more apparent.

Determined to solve the puzzle, we decided to enlist our friend Charlotte, who was a nurse specializing in newborn care. She agreed to come over early on the next Saturday, before Jessica woke up, and observe the twitching and twisting that had by now become a normal part of her waking routine.

Sure enough, right on schedule there was the subtle twitching and twisting with a slight head turn and stiffening at the end.

Charlotte was very quiet as she took notes.

"I don't want to frighten you, or alarm you, but what I am observing would, or at least could be considered, some kind of seizure activity," she said to us gently, *"...that doesn't mean it is anything to be concerned about at this point, but you need to keep an eye on it."*

She smiled reassuringly.

We explained to Charlotte that we had mentioned it to the doctor and he wasn't concerned. Since we had a 'well baby' check-up coming up in December, she instructed us to keep a daily journal of our observations to give to the doctor at our next appointment.

We began a log of baby Jessica's behavior the very next day, and after a week or so, there was no doubt. Something odd was going on with her and it was not going away.

With a distinct sense of dread, we kept our little notes and hid our fears in our hearts, as we prepared for our next appointment with our doctor.

We had to solve this mystery. We had to wake up from what was looking more and more like our worst nightmare.

We didn't want to speak it, but, something seemed to be dreadfully wrong with our little Jessica.

An Unforgettable Visit from...

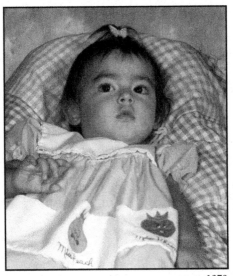

1978

...the Terror of the Unknown.

Chapter 5

An unforgettable visit from... the terror of the unknown.

There is an old classic science fiction movie about a man from outer space who lands on earth with a mission to force the world to put down their atomic weapons and live in peace. Of course he was rejected and persecuted. So to make his point, he did something that struck terror into the hearts of the 'earthlings' and really got their attention. It was called 'The Day the Earth Stood Still.' He made his point in an unforgettable way.

December 29, 1978 was the day 'our world' stood still and we will never forget it.

We had an appointment with our family doctor on that day. It was on the last Friday in December, just before the big New Year's Day weekend. Because of our concerns about Jessica's strange spells, which we had carefully documented, I had taken the afternoon off from work to go with Renée to Jessica's four month check-up.

We marched in there fueled by our concerns and armed with the little journal of our baby's strange behavior. A lengthy discussion followed, and no matter what we said, the doctor persisted, over and over reassuring us that all was well and it was probably nothing more than a stage she was going through that would disappear as she matured.

He could see no reason for concern, and looking back now at his notes on Jessica's check up that morning, he makes no note of our discussions. Only that she was a 'well baby'. There is no mention of our concerns. At the end of the meeting we went down the hall and Jessica received her second DPT shot and then we went home, feeling somewhat relieved by the doctor's confident assurance that *"...all is well."*

The terror of the unknown was there, waiting for us.

Renée was quietly nursing Jessica, sitting on a stool at the breakfast bar in our kitchen. It was always a very special time of closeness for her and her new little girl.

We were both relieved after the visit to the doctor's office and we looked forward to the long fun holiday weekend with our family. Life was good and we were at peace, feeling safe and warm together, as we looked out at the snowy, late December afternoon.

Suddenly, without warning, sheer terror struck!

Renée screamed in fright in a way that I had never heard before, and as I whirled around I could see Jessica in her arms jerking and twisting violently and then suddenly going limp... her eyes half open and rolled back in her head, her skin was as white as death, and above Jessica's limp and hanging form I could see Renée's trance-like wide-eyed stare, as if to say... *'This can't be happening!'*

Time stood still... our world had stopped turning. It was so quiet. I remember I could hear the clock... tick...tick... ticking... in the background.

I grabbed Jessica in my arms and tried to arouse her... there was no response... her head was flopping limply. I laid her on the breakfast bar and began to massage her, pinch her, poke her. She looked dead and was completely unresponsive. I remember her skin felt strangely cold and clammy.

I continued to work feverishly on her. I pressed on her chest and pulled her arms up to help her breathe... and time slipped slowly by... nothing... nothing... not breathing... *'she is gone!'* I thought. But I couldn't stop... I wouldn't stop! This couldn't be happening!

All of this couldn't have taken more than a minute or two maximum, but it seemed like an eternity! I am sure I was holding my breath and trying to will her to breathe again.

As I worked on her, suddenly with a jerk, she took a gasping breath and then another, the color returned to her face and her eyes opened... she was still alive! I took a deep breath.

I looked at the clock... it was 2:40 pm. I quickly grabbed the phone and called the doctor's office. As the seconds ticked by while I waited for the nurse to answer, Jessica looked more and more normal. It was so very surreal.

"We have had a problem with our little girl Jessica and we are coming back to see the doctor!" I said with feeling and probably a little louder than necessary.

Something in my voice made my point. *"Okay,"* the nurse said meekly, *"...we are very busy and you may have to wait a long time."*

"I don't care how long we have to wait. We are going to see the doctor today!" I said.

I hung up the phone and turned to Renée, who by now had cuddled Jessica in her arms and was staring at me with a tear stained face. Her expression said what I was thinking. Something was wrong, terribly wrong with Jessica, but what was it?

I remember how physically suffocating the fear of the unknown felt at that moment. My heart was thumping hard.

And so the terrible mystery was upon us, and our little world had begun to wobble out of control. With a sense of foreboding we hurriedly loaded up for our second trip to the doctor's office on that fateful day... December 29, 1978.

From that day forward, nothing would ever be the same.

The Mystery Begins...

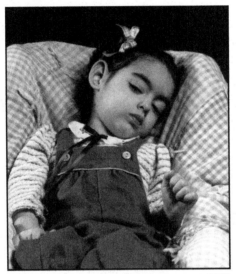

1978

...Off into the Void.

Chapter 6

The mystery begins... off into the void.

We sat quietly waiting in the lobby of the medical center, watching a steady stream of coughing, sniffing children pass in front of us. It was now nearly 7 pm.

Sitting there, feeling very alone on our own little island, we had been waiting for almost four hours. The routine had become monotonous... staring at little Jessica who was sleeping in her baby carrier at our feet... a furtive glance up when the nurse would appear to call the next patient... a glimmer of hope and then disappointment... a glance at each other and then back to watching our baby.

Jessica looked so perfectly normal as we looked at her peacefully dozing, her long curly eyelashes and gentle breathing made the experience of a few hours ago seem like a very distant nightmare. Maybe... just maybe... there was a chance... but, no... the reality of the horror I had witnessed was seared in my mind, like nothing I had ever seen. Even today as I write this, many years later, the pain I felt then, comes flooding back as I force myself to re-live the experience.

"Jessica Walker?" I jumped, as the tired sounding voice of our doctor's nurse, interrupted my thoughts.

We gathered Jessica up, and headed through the door, down the hallway to the examining room that we had left just hours before, but, this time, Renée, Jessica and I were different people. We had stepped out of our comfortable little world, into an unknown and apparently dangerous new one.

The lines of fatigue were clearly showing on our doctor's face as he listened to our recounting of the afternoon's events, occasionally nodding, sometimes looking skeptical or puzzled. Then, as we finished, he sat there silently.

It was very, very quiet in the room. My heart was thumping hard as I waited for him to speak.

After what seemed like an eternity, the doctor cleared his throat, shrugged and began to speak, *"...uhmm, well you know.. Jessica is very young and ...well, babies do some funny things."* He stood and moved toward the door with a shrug, *"It's most likely nothing to be concerned about,"* he said, as he continued toward the door, his hand reaching for the knob.

In my mind, I was replaying everything: Renée's terrifying scream... the jerking... the paleness... the whites of Jessica's eyes showing through her half open eyelids... the smell of death. I stepped in front of the doctor and shut the door.

Our eyes met and I couldn't help noticing the startled look on his face. It was the moment of truth and we were going to find the answer! I had to know what was going on.

"Listen to me doctor! We are not panicky parents. As you know, we have two other children. We have seen a lot, and been through sickness with them, and I am telling you, there is something terribly wrong... with Jessica!" In my mind I flinched at those words. I had finally said it. My heart dropped to my feet.

"You were not there," I continued. *"...you did not see what I just saw. It was not pretty. It was the worst thing I have ever seen.*

I don't have a word to describe it. I don't know what it is, but... there is something very wrong with this kid!" I said passionately.

The pain I was feeling in my heart was unbearable. I waited in silence for a reply from the doctor, who stood frozen in his tracks, his hand still reaching for the door.

The doctor stepped back. He was watching my face carefully. A sigh, a shrug and then with a condescending tone to his voice he said, *"Okay. Okay,"* he sighed, *"The only thing we can do is to send Jessica to a specialist, you know... a neurologist."*

A neurologist? I turned that over in my mind. That was a brain doctor. Was he saying that Jessica's brain was damaged in some way? A sobering thought.

"We probably won't find anything, but if it will make you feel better, I will schedule it." Rubbing his eyes absentmindedly, he went on, *"Realize that the neuro clinic has a huge backlog of cases. You will probably have to wait at least 3 to 6 months."*

"I don't care how long it takes or who we have to see, just make the call." I said.

'We were not giving up,' I thought, 'We will never give up! We will find out what's wrong and we will fix it and our little world will return to it's orbit!' I was determined, because I believed that somehow, somewhere, the answer was waiting.

But, in the meantime, we would do everything we could to help Jessica. I thought of Charlotte's quiet comment, *"...some kind of seizure activity."* I shuddered at the implication of that. No doubt about it, we were heading into uncharted waters.

I looked at Renée and she was looking at me, as she sat there with Jessica in her lap. I noticed the tears in her eyes and the slightly hopeful look on her face. We had begun the fight to return to a normal life. We were committed.

Little did we know what lay before us.

A greater question was forming in my mind. '*Why was this happening to Jessica?*'

That night the doctor wrote in Jessica's medical record, "*...examination unremarkable today...*" and then, "*...although I think that a consultation with a neurologist would be appropriate.*"

And so we scheduled the appointment that night, and off we went into the void, desperately hoping for answers.

The Storms of Fear & Uncertainty...

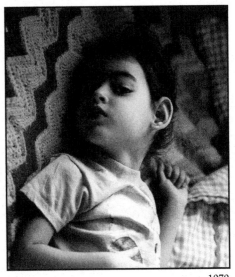

1979

...A Small Miracle.

Growing Up with JESSICA

Chapter 7

The storms of fear and uncertainty...
a small miracle.

Early the next week, following the events on that traumatic Friday, our phone rang.

Renée answered. *"Hello, Mrs. Walker, this is the Neuro Clinic calling..."* the voice said, *"...due to a cancellation, we have an opening sooner than we expected."* In amazement, Renée struggled to respond.

When we had left the doctor's office on Friday, December 29, the crisp winter air felt just a little colder, the wind more penetrating, and the night darker than it had ever been. We were full of uncertainty, the unknown was looming, and our little world was sailing into an ever widening orbit.

We were struggling with our emotions and doubts and the uncertainty of the situation...

'*What was wrong?*'

'*Would Jessica be okay?*'

'*Why was this happening?*'

Our hearts were full of fear and uncertainty that night, as we returned home emotionally spent.

Renée and I agreed, as we talked it over, that waiting for three or maybe as long as six months would be exquisite torture.

The four hour wait we had just endured in the doctor's waiting room had seemed like an eternity. How would we ever stand it? I remember the fear of the unknown was so tangible, I could feel it pressing down on top of us.

We turned to our faith in God.

Our faith had grown from the first week of our married life thirteen years before, as we started reading the Bible together every night. We weren't very sophisticated about it. We just started at the front and read all the way to the back.

Renée had made a serious commitment to Christ when she was a teenager, but I knew very little about such things, although I had some 'church' experience in my grade school years. I was pretty clueless. I can say though, I was honestly curious about the deeper things of life.

We both had Christian friends who had encouraged us and invited us to church, Sunday School classes and get togethers. The second year we were married we were given tickets to a Billy Graham film by Menno Kliewer, the father of a friend. And so we went, not knowing what to expect.

At the end of that film I had gone forward and prayed to receive Christ. My heart exploded with joy and I really did feel the reality of God. I had discovered what was missing in my life. I no longer felt alone.

I was very much an intellectual skeptic, and I began to study and learn everything I could. An important book was *'Evidence that*

Demands a Verdict' by Josh McDowell. After a few years, I eventually became a Sunday School teacher for young marrieds.

At about that time, I had heard about Dr. James Dobson, the Christian Psychologist. He had written a book called *'Dare to Discipline'* on the subject of rearing children using Christian principles, and a second book, *'Hide or Seek',* on the topic of developing your child's 'self esteem.'

We attended a conference lead by Dr. Dobson and we devoured everything with a passion and applied it to our lives. We grew closer as a couple and grew in our faith.

Those two authors were a great and positive impact on Renée and me. Our church and our pastor were inspiring and supportive as were our Christian friends.

When we had arrived home that day, we had spent a lot of time on the phone sharing with our little network of friends and we asked them all to pray for us. We needed to see the neurologist now! That was the essence of our prayer request and the word went out, and many people began to pray for us.

"*I know this is short notice,*" the calm voice continued, "*...but could you come this Wednesday morning?*" ...she paused, waiting for a response.

Renée still couldn't believe her ears. "*You mean this week? ...this Wednesday?*" She finally said breathlessly.

"*Yes. Is that too soon?*" said the voice.

"NO! We'll be there," Renée answered, *"We WILL be there!"*

Renée hung up the phone in stunned silence. Our prayers had been answered in a very dramatic and merciful way! It seemed too good to be true.

Her heart was overflowing with thankfulness and relief.

As she went and stood over Jessica's peacefully sleeping form, with a weak smile, in a way that only a mother could feel, she thought to herself, *'We will find out what is wrong and whatever it is, we will fix it, and my baby will be okay...*

...Jessica will be okay!'

She smiled again, with complete and utter relief.

I am sure that if cellular phones had been invented then, mine would have been ringing off the hook, as I was driving home at that moment. Shortly afterwards I walked in the door and one look at Renée's face told me something great had happened.

It was nothing, really... just a small miracle!

The Marathon Begins...

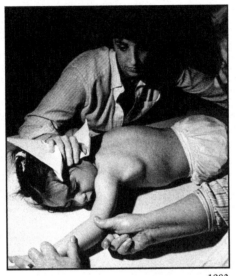

1983

...No End in Sight.

Chapter 8

The marathon begins... no end in sight.

The word 'marathon' comes from the story of a Greek warrior who ran home from the battlefield, over 26 miles, to bring the message of victory. After delivering the victorious news, so the story goes, he collapsed and died on the spot.

So I guess the race itself can kill.

We didn't really know or understand that we were entering into our very own personal marathon. The difference was that we were looking for 'victory,' not singing its praises.

The days leading up to our appointment at the Neuro Clinic, passed in a blur of both excitement and anticipation. It was good to be moving forward, to be hopeful that life would become normal once again and all would, or at least could, be well again.

Having never faced anything as forbiddingly unknown as we now faced, I think Renée and I had kind of an optimistic faith in modern medicine to cure anything that came our way. Doctors and other medical experts were up there on the pedestal of *'All-knowing and all powerful,' and* there was nothing they couldn't cure. We were very naive.

We had of course immediately called our friend Charlotte. *"Would she be willing to accompany us, to help interpret the findings we were sure to discover?"*

She quickly agreed to go with us to see the neurologist. Later we would be very thankful we had asked her.

The big day dawned brightly and the recent heavy snowfall began to melt, as the day turned into a rather balmy, sunny day for early January. We bundled Jessica up and headed down to our 8:30 am appointment. We had kept her up as late as possible the night before, as they had instructed us, so that she would sleep through her 'EEG.' We would be testing her brain functions.

'*Electroencephalogram*,' or EEG, was another new term for us. It was something we had vaguely heard of but had never experienced. It basically measures ongoing electrical activity in the brain. The measurements are accomplished by placing a number of electrodes, actually pasting them, on a patients head, and the result is graphed on a slow moving sheet of continuous paper with a pen for each set of measurement points.

We watched silently with a lump in our throat, as the technician methodically pasted what looked like rubber suction cups with a wire attached, to Jessica's tiny head.

She lay there looking as normal as apple pie, breathing slowly as she slept, in her tiny pink chiffon dress. The machine began to gently hum as paper cascaded slowly through the printer.

Suddenly I realized I was holding my breath.

Later, Renée, Charlotte and I sat waiting in Doctor William's office, trying not to fidget. I was hopeful, but I couldn't shake the memories of that Friday afternoon when everything had changed. Somehow I knew, although it was difficult to speak it, that something was, or had gone terribly wrong with little Jessica.

The '*blessed one*' I thought. How ironic. I was braced for the worst, although I hadn't really expressed my fears to anyone else.

I had already commited in my mind that I would do everything I could to get to the 'cure' or whatever Jessica needed.

I could sense a marathon of doctors, medicine, tests and machines awaiting us and perhaps we should give her therapy so that... the door quickly opened, interrupting my thoughts. I looked up into the somber face of Doctor Williams.

He cleared his throat and began to speak the words I will never forget. *"Well, I will get right to the point. Your daughter is having brain seizures..."* there was that word again, *"...some observable, but in any case, up to five seizures per second."* He paused, glanced at us both, and then continued, *"... and I guess I don't know why!"*

So! There it was.

The doctor's words had a numbing effect. I looked at Charlotte, she smiled in a comforting way and asked the Doctor several questions. I looked at Renée. She was frozen, her eyes wide as she grappled with this new information. My heart ached for her. I knew what she must be feeling, because I felt it too. This was really happening!

"I am recommending we do some more testing," the doctor said hopefully, sensing the impact of his words, *"...there's a new type of brain x-ray called a 'CAT Scan.' It means 'computerized axial tomography.' It is completely painless and quick and maybe it will give us a clue, as far as what we are dealing with..."* his voice trailed off.

I looked at Renée, and as our eyes met, I could see the shock and pain on her face. *"Okay."* I said, *"Let's do it as soon as possible!"*

We needed to do something, I thought. Anything and everything!

We gathered Jessica up in awkward silence, and after a few polite thank you's we headed home. I dropped everyone off at home and headed straight for the library. I was feeling a little dizzy with all of this. 'EEG's, 'brain seizures,' 'CAT scans.'
I needed to know what we were up against.

'What were brain 'seizures?'

'What were the implications of a child with 'brain seizures?'

I had to have some answers.

As I looked in the 'subject index' in the card catalog at our local library under 'seizures,' a familiar name popped up. 'Dr. James Dobson'. Apparently, before he began to write and teach about Christian-based child rearing, Dr. Dobson, who is a clinical psychologist, had co-authored a book on mental retardation, with a section on 'Seizures and Epilepsy.' I was comforted by seeing his name. A name I knew and trusted. I found the book and began to read.

The marathon was beginning for real, and I could see no end ...no end in sight.

Two Different Perspectives...

1984

...Dark Clouds on the Horizon.

Growing Up with JESSICA

Chapter 9

Two different perspectives... dark clouds on the horizon.

Renée's parents divorced when she was about three and she spent
a number of years in foster homes separated from her father and
brother.

During that time in her life she began having re-occurring
nightmares about her alcoholic mother. Her mother had
actually kidnapped her when she was a child... more than once.
These disturbing dreams would continue to haunt her clear up
through her high school years.

When she was at last reunited with her father and brother,
shaken and insecure, she felt that she had to prove herself
worthy of their love. With a child's tender faith, her first prayer
was, *"Please God, don't let anything happen to my daddy!"*

Renée resolved in her heart to be the perfect daughter and
sister and to never give anyone a reason not to love her.

When we met, married and started our family, she extended her
resolve to be the *'perfect'* wife and mother. Remembering her
painful past, she had fixed in her mind the idea that she would be
the ideal loving mother, who would nourish her little children
and protect them from all harm. Then Jessica entered our lives,
and she found herself facing the ultimate challenge.

As Jessica's life turned more and more away from the normal, the
demons of Renée's past returned to haunt her. Her world was

beginning to unravel and there was very little she could do to control it. This was an all too familiar feeling and she was slowly devastated. We moved through a constant world of doctors and tests and puzzled looks and exhaustion. When would this be over? She couldn't bear the thought.

Jessica lay sleeping calmly in the jaws of the enormous CAT scan machinery. She looked so very normal lying there in the dimly lit room, wearing her little pink dress, white frilly socks and patent leather shoes. There was a slight clicking sound and a bright red cross-hair appeared from above, centered on her tiny forehead. Then, a slight whirring could be heard as her metallic bed moved imperceptibly. The whole scene was once again very surreal like a bad science fiction movie... but all too real.

Renée's head was spinning with a torrent of emotions as she watched from a distance. In her mind she thought, *'What has happened... this can't be real... there can't be anything seriously wrong... I refuse to believe it!'* And in the background, the massive machine continued to click... pause... whirr... click... pause... whirr... and her heart sank lower and lower, and the panic, fear and insecurity of her youth, began to seep slowly back into her heart.

With a mother's optimism she had assumed that we would find the answer and settle on a solution. Probably some miracle of modern medicine, and all would be well again. A long term disability in her precious little Jessica was not an option and it just couldn't happen.

The CAT scan was completely normal.

There was *"No abnormality, no damage, her brain appears normal in every way,"* the doctor said, as we peered at the x-rays of her upper skull and brain. *"I see no possible physical cause for her seizures,"* a phrase that would be repeated over and over again as the years inched by. *"Nothing remarkable to report,"* he said, matter-of-factly.

As I stared at the images of Jessica's head, photographically sliced in quarter inch sections, like a loaf of bread, from the top down to her petite little nose. I couldn't help but think to myself, *'Wow, just to be able to look inside her head so easily, without pain or surgery. That is 'remarkable' in itself!'*

I don't know why, but I have always been able to keep calm in a crisis. Everything kind of slows down and I can think very calmly towards my next move.

As I assisted the nurse in my lead apron that day, I watched Jessica sleeping and thought to myself, *'Maybe we will figure this mystery out, but it may take awhile. Yet on the other hand, maybe this is it! Maybe Jessica's beyond help. It could be too late.'* I glanced up at Renée waiting in the control booth. I thought I could see tears in her eyes.

My mind was calmly checking off our options, *'We needed to do something; actually everything possible, to preserve whatever it was that Jessica had left, until we could find the answer; therapy or whatever was needed, as we continued the search, in the months and maybe years ahead.'*

'This wasn't going to be easy,' I thought.

I resolved to fight to the finish, starting right now.

At that same moment as she watched through the glass, Renée's mind was spinning. She was not fully comprehending what all of this might mean and she was feeling more and more helpless.

'I can't go on like this,' she thought.

The difference in our perspectives would become critical. We were pointing in different directions and surely heading for a major crisis.

As I look back now, I realize that I didn't see the dark clouds gathering. I just didn't understand the depth of Renée's despair.

Something had to give.

Hitting the Wall...

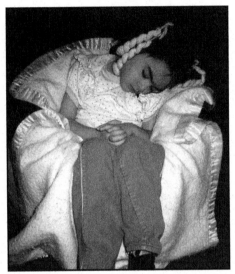

1980's

...Denial & Anger.

Growing Up with JESSICA

Chapter 10

Hitting the wall... denial and anger.

Renée is a very loving and special person and it was frustrating to see her suffer so deeply. The *'perfect'* life that she had wanted and worked towards, was slowly and inevitably spinning out of control. She was like a top that was starting to wobble... a sure sign of the crash that was coming. As the tests mounted and the list of medical experts grew with the same puzzling results and no sure answers, the panic mounted in her heart and soul. *'Why? Why was this happening?'*

In her mind she was crying out to God.

'No! NO! Lord, how could you allow this to happen?'

I guess you could say she was in denial, refusing to believe what was becoming slowly more obvious. Jessica might never recover from this mysterious ailment. To consider that Jessica's problems were permanent was just too much for her.

Eventually, guilt began to take hold of her, as she asked herself the old questions, stoked by her painful childhood memories of rejection by her own mother...

> *'What have I done?'*

> *'Lord, why are you punishing me?'*

> *'How have I failed You?'*

As Renée was sucked deeper into despair, Jessica began several forms of therapy, sometimes alone, other times with other handicapped and retarded children. As she became acquainted with the whole scene she told herself, *'Jessica is not abnormal... she doesn't belong here!'* She was feeling increasingly desperate.

Her despondency made even the simplest tasks seem insurmountable. She became more unengaged with our other children. She was unable to function as a loving wife and mother. She was trapped in a nightmare and she couldn't wake up.

As time crawled slowly by in the seemly endless routine of therapy and doctors and genetic tests and more tests and more puzzled expressions, she was feeling more and more emotionally drained, and then her anger showed up!

She was feeling abandoned by God and became increasingly angry at Him. She actually became frightened of Jessica and confused and overwhelmed by her baby's grim future.

Not sure she had the courage to cope, she began to retreat from everything she held dear... her family and friends... church... and most importantly of all from God.

As her husband, I tried to reach her, to help her and counsel her, but she shut me out. Perhaps even resenting me, because I was able to cope, and she wasn't. I guess in retrospect I didn't know how to help her or what to say. I just didn't see the breadth and depth of the problem.

Finally, one day at dinner, our son Jon, reached for his milk, and as children sometimes do, he knocked it over on the table and it ran everywhere! Renée exploded into a furious anger, crying with anguish as she scolded him.

Jon looked at her, dazed by her outburst, with tears in his eyes.

A new crisis was upon us!

Stunned, as I looked at them, the gravity of the whole situation began to crystallize in my mind.

I could clearly see now, the size of Renée's anguish and pain. I had been so focused on solving the problem with Jessica, that I had been blinded to how much deeper this was hurting Renée. I felt a rush of empathy for her... I had been so very blind!

It now seemed so obvious. I felt like I had let her down.

It is undeniable, that there is an incredible link between a mother and her child that transcends understanding. I came to grips with it that day. What I had overlooked was the total empathy between them, as Jessica struggled and was racked with seizures. Renée was living it out in her own heart, and yet felt so powerless to stop it.

As I looked at her that day, I could now see a scared little girl caught in a painful nightmare that seemingly had no end.

Renée was at the end of her *'endurance.'*

She was *'hitting the wall'* with full force.

I had to help her... but how?

Growing Up with JESSICA

The Comfort of
Trusting God...

1980's

...Letting
Go.

Chapter 11

The comfort of trusting God... letting go.

I felt as much to blame as anything else for Renée's now obvious misery. It was time for outside help. We needed someone who could reach her. It had to be someone who could get her back on course, and as I thought it over, I knew just the person.

Rachel, was the wife of the assistant pastor at our church, and there was no doubt she had a calming *'big sister'* kind of effect on Renée. I was sure that Rachel could help as I turned over in my mind the many examples of their relationship and the mutual love and respect between them. Renée needed to talk to someone like her, and I knew Rachel would be loving but tough, and would unselfishly go the extra mile if need be.

I wasn't sure how to approach Renée about it.

The direct approach seemed right.

When we were alone and could talk freely, I sat down with Renée and looked her straight in the eye.

I said to her, *"I think you have two choices."* I hesitated, looking deeply into her tender brown eyes. I could see the tears welling up and the lines of pain in her face.

I wondered how I could have been so completely blind to her now very obvious anguish and pain.

"Either you get in the car and go see Rachel or..." I swallowed

hard and took a deep breath, *"...I will put you in the car and take you over there."* I was desperate.

She dropped her gaze and said, *"Okay... okay, you're right. I need help. I have questions... I... okay, okay... I will call her and see if she can see me as soon as possible."*

And so, her recovery started that very day.

Renée and Rachel shared together, they prayed together, and they cried together. They began to meet every week and Renée began to turn around almost immediately.

She came home with assignments from Rachel. Things to do with each of us. Renée began spending time alone with each of our other children, slowly beginning again, to appreciate and cherish her family... Jamie and Jon... and don't forget Jim.

She was no longer frightened of Jessica. In fact, it was at that time that we all grew closer together and closer to Jessica and she became our *'very special child',* our *'blessed one'.* We had never been more at peace.

At last, Renée was able to completely give Jessica up to God. The deeper meaning of her middle name, *'consecrated to God,'* was truly fulfilled then, as it remains to this very day.

We had learned an important lesson in spite of our tragedy.

The God that Renée had met as a high schooler, and I had met at the age of 20, was still there loving us unconditionally.

We knew we had put too much faith in our own ability and the knowledge and ability of our doctors and their limited and finite power. Our faith in God had set us free. Even though we were beginning to find the measure of the life before us, we no longer feared the future.

There was an indescribable joy that is difficult to describe, in the comfort of learning to trust God in our sorrows .

We now knew, that no matter what the future would bring, we would be all right. Life in our little world was much brighter and we knew that we could love Jessica unconditionally, just like God loved us.

Now we treasured even more greatly, the three children, that had blessed our lives.

This whole disaster had taught us a valuable and critical lesson... a lesson that we would dearly treasure and cling to over and over, in the dark days ahead.

Jessica was at last, truly 'consecrated to God.'

Growing Up with JESSICA

Staggering Forward...

1978

...the Impact on Our Family.

Chapter 12

Staggering forward... the impact on our family.

What do you do when you are faced with a situation that has no easy solution?

No *'quick fix.'*

No *'medical breakthrough.'*

No *'miracle'* cure.

No *'diagnosis.'*

No *'explanation.'*

You talk to dozens of doctors and specialists and get the same puzzled looks and quizzical expressions, usually followed by, "*Well, she certainly is a mystery.*" There was no end in sight.

What would you do?

Here's what we did. We staggered forward.

We knew that Jessica *'the blessed one'* was a very special person loved by God, and we loved her all the more tenderly as the years passed by.

Renée and I and our children, Jamie and Jon, formed a ferocious bond of love with this petite little girl who does not speak, nor in her early years, even sit up or roll around.

We could sense her strong little spirit behind her disabilities, and we showered her with our love and attention. I think it could be said that, if love could cure her she would be cured. And this mysterious little stranger gave us many unforgettable lessons in *'unselfish love.'*

All the while Jessica endured the tests and probing and poking, and the days inched slowly by, turning into months and the months into years. We staggered forward, growing closer and closer together, helping each other cope, holding on tight and trusting the wisdom of God.

Our friends and our faith in God comforted us and we went slowly forward, measuring Jessica's progress in the minutest of terms. *"I think she looked... noticed... reached out to me... today!"* Her life was in perpetual slow motion.

Of course, the *'search'* continued unabated for the mysterious villain that had harmed her, and we never stopped looking for the answer. Sometimes, when we were exhausted mentally and physically we felt like quitting. Then one look into Jessica's eyes, and sharing a look with her, was all it took to keep going and going and going.

When you have a handicapped or *'special'* child sometimes in your dreams at night you see her running and laughing and playing and the joy in your heart is indescribable. When you wake up, you go to where your child is sleeping and with tears running down your cheeks, you just sit and watch and marvel at what might have been .

Loving a child like Jessica is a sometimes bittersweet experience.

The pain is there, yet the day by day victories and defeats enrich your life in amazing ways. You *'grow up'* as you go forward.

Little things happen that are kind of glimmers of the beauty of the experience.

I remember my son Jon, when he was playing football, sometimes arriving late for practice because he was baby sitting his *'little sister'.* As you can imagine he was razzed a little by the other kids, but especially by one of the coaches who ridiculed him and teased him. Jon never mentioned this to us, even though it must have been humiliating to him personally. He endured it for us and for Jessica... a rather unselfish and very mature act for a ten year old.

When I found out at the end of the year at the football banquet, what had been going on, I rolled Jessica up to the coach in her wheelchair and said to him, *"This is Jon's little sister, do you have any questions?"* Blushing, he mumbled his apologies.

As a result a burly football coach was given a lesson in unselfish love by a ten year old and a three year old handicapped little girl. I ask you, who was the one with the real handicap?

I recall another time that I was feeling a little down and not coping very well with things in general. In my dismay, I locked myself in my home office.

Not one of my better moments, you might say.

My daughter Jamie who was about twelve, slipped a note under my door, it read, *'Dear Dad, I love you. I am sorry you are feeling bad. Please unlock the door. I miss you. Love, Jamie.'*

Another lesson in love and compassion. I kept that note for years.

Jessica has never spoken one word, and yet she has written volumes across our hearts and the hearts of everyone who knows us.

When we have shared the fact, (with those people who know us) that I am writing this book to share with others, they often breakdown and cry. It is a mysterious thing, and a marvel to me. It gives me a much bigger perspective on life in '*Jessica-land*.'

The impact of little Jessica on all of us, is immeasurable. I am sure it is a bigger impact on the world than I have made in my entire life of working and striving.

God really does work in mysterious and wondrous ways. I know because everyday I look into the eyes of one of His little masterpieces, the '*blessed one*,' that is '*consecrated to God*.'... dear sweet Jessica.

It takes my breath away.

Mind-Numbing
Anxiety...

1984

...Gasping for
Breath.

Chapter 13

Mind-numbing anxiety... gasping for breath.

When I was growing up, I was always small for my age, until I hit Junior High. Suddenly I exploded, and grew to my present height of six feet. My classmates took note of the change and voted me 'legs' of my class. A dubious 'honor' since along with the growth came clumsiness and many awkward moments and even pain in my legs. Nothing more than 'growing pains' I was told, and eventually I stopped growing, and the pain stopped.

Although we have all grown pretty steadily in our faith and love through this experience over the years, we have experienced our share of what I would call 'growing pains.' It does hurt to grow but growth is ultimately good.

There were many painful 'growth' incidents I remember, but there is one that really stands out.

I had parked out in front of our house and walked up the sidewalk. I was feeling great, whistling softly to myself. Things were going well. I looked forward to sharing the excitement I was feeling with Renée.

I was smiling as I reached for the door handle.

I had taken a second job, hoping to move into a position where I could leave the corporate world behind, and work from home. And help Renée full time, with the never ending care for Jessica and our young children. I wanted our lives to be as normal as possible, and Renée deserved to be released from as much of the responsibility as possible. Not that we hadn't shared the burdens from the beginning, but I had learned a hard lesson from her near collapse, and I wanted to lighten her burden as much as possible.

She deserved to be happy and spend time with our two other delightful children. I needed to be there for her. Once again, Jessica's quiet influence was shaping the course of our lives.

I paused in the doorway, a half frozen smile on my lips, transfixed by what confronted me. Renée was sitting in the middle of the floor, looking very pale, holding a limp Jessica to her chest and slowly rocking back and forth. *"Jessica is having trouble breathing,"* she said in a hoarse whisper.

When you raise a child like Jessica, it is fraught with what might be called 'secondary' health risks. Because she is in a compromised health condition, she can become susceptible to a variety of ailments. Compounding that, was the fact that she had numerous seizures daily, both observable and below the surface.

One of the things we had learned, was that when a brain seizure occurs, a large amount of saliva is released, which has to go somewhere. It can be swallowed, drooled, or 'aspirated.'

To 'aspirate' is to basically breathe the liquid into your lungs, similar to when you are drinking something and accidentally choke. In Jessica's case, this 'choking' hazard was constantly lurking there, in the background of every activity.

'Eating' is another hazard which occurs a minimum of three times daily. Realize, that seizures are unpredictable in their frequency, intensity and duration. I like to use the analogy of *'lightning strikes'.* Seizures are kind of like lightning strikes in the central nervous system, and are very sporadic and unpredictable. And so, as you can imagine, they can occur in mid-bite or while swallowing, or at any time. So we have another risk to negotiate daily.

In Jessica's case, this was compounded by her petite size and the dainty size of her airway passages including her lungs and bronchial tubes. Smaller air passages equal greater risk.

Quite predictably, in spite of our close observation and quick response to any problem, she was hospitalized with 'URI' or Upper Respiratory Infection, numerous times.

Only hours before, I had been playing on the floor with Jessica. She was perfectly normal, or at least normal for her condition and the influence of her seizure medication.

I contrasted all of that with what I was seeing. No doubt about it, this was the worst one yet.

Kneeling to look at Jessica, I noted that she looked very pale, much like that fateful Friday nearly seven years earlier. This time though, her breathing echoed around the room... wheeze.... gasp... wheeze... gasp... wheeze... a very long pause and then... gaaasp!

I touched her cheek. She was on fire.

I listened to Renée's trembling account of what had happened. Jessica had been a little lethargic and so she had been watching her closely. Renée seems to have sixth sense on these things. She can just feel it coming. A fact that had probably saved, and continues to save Jessica, to this day. I trusted Renée's account completely.

Not 20 or 30 minutes before I walked in the door, Jessica had suddenly taken a turn for the worse. Her temperature began to shoot up, while her breathing quickly deteriorated .

This was something very viral, I thought. Perhaps a quick pneumonia. Now was the time for action. I bundled her up and headed for the car. Renée stood up still trembling. *"I can't go with you,"* she sobbed. *"After the last time, I don't think I can handle it."*

I understood. *"It's okay,"* I said gently. *"Please call the hospital."*

The last time we had a problem with Jessica and another 'URI', we had rushed into the hospital emergency room and confronted a doctor we had never met before. He had looked at Jessica quickly, and catching Renée in his scornful gaze, he said with disgust, *"This child is very sick... VERY sick!"* She caught his implication immediately and rushed from the room in tears.

Surprised and shocked at his behavior, I set him straight in a hurry, but the damage had been done. Renée was extremely hurt that he would accuse her of anything close to neglect.

I understood why she now recoiled at the thought.

In her hurting heart and soul, Renée was pleading, *'This is the worst one ever! I can't bear the thought of her dying in my arms. Oh, please Lord... help me!'*

I put Jessica on the seat next to me where I could touch her little chest. I slammed the car into gear and raced off towards the hospital.

Fortunately, the hospital emergency room is just straight down a main street about five miles from our house, and it was about 10:45 pm, back then in our home town, a relatively quiet time. Green light or red light, I never stopped at all, as I raced at top speed through the darkness. One hand on Jessica, feeling her breathe... gasp... wheeze... a pause... I waited for the next gasp... waiting... waiting... in alarm I pressed on her chest... at last a long ragged gasp.

I screeched to a halt in the glaring lights of the hospital emergency room entrance. As I looked up, I could see the staff coming my way. They had received Renée's call.

"Mrs. Walker, this is the emergency room doctor at St. Luke's." Renée listened, holding her breath. *"We have Jessica here..."* her knees felt weak, as she gasped for the air to answer.

"...we have stabilized her and she is doing fine. She is going to be hospitalized for a while, but she's okay!"

Renée hung up the phone and sank slowly to the floor.

At that same moment, I sat there in the emergency room, now feeling completely numb with anxiety. I watched Jessica breathing peacefully. I couldn't get the sound of her gasping for breath, just minutes before, out of my head.

I heard the doctor speaking behind me, *"...she' okay!"*

Renée sat on the kitchen floor with her back against the wall, her eyes closed. *"Thank you Lord,"* she whispered numbly, *"Thank you,"* as visions of Jessica filled her head, and gratefulness flooded her heart. *"Thank you."*

I guess I would conclude, that these kind of experiences really did hurt a lot at the time, and I wouldn't have chosen them, but looking back now, I realize that without the pain there would have been no growth.

As I said before... *'growth is good.'*

The 'Mystery'...

1980's

...Begins to Unravel.

Growing Up with JESSICA

Chapter 14

The mystery... begins to unravel.

A wise sage once said, *"Doctors are like plumbers, some are real artists of their trade, while others... well, let's just say, their pipes leak."* After consulting and working with over 60 medical experts and doctors in the first two to three years of Jessica's life, I would have to agree, it is a mixed bag.

Members of the medical profession, in my mind, are no longer up there on a pedestal. They are not infallible.

There are, however, some very unselfish and dedicated people out there. Some of them very bright. One such is Dr. Robert C. Burton, or as he once said to us *"Not the actor, you know, I am the other one."* He was a delightfully humorous and refreshing personality and an absolutely brilliant neurologist.

Dr. Burton was the founding partner at Neurology Associates, coincidently the very same practice who had, through Dr. Williams, done Jessica's first EEG. He had also been the Director of Children's Medicine at the MAYO clinic for more than a decade.

When other neurologists would go to a seminar, Dr. Burton was one of the people they were going to hear speak. He once had made medical history by determining that rabies had been transmitted in an eye cornea transplant, against all odds and in spite of the skepticism of his contemporaries. It was the *first time* such a thing had ever happened or at least was correctly diagnosed. He was an uninhibited and thinker not affected by prevailing medical biases. He became one of the vital keys to our solution of the 'Jessica mystery' and an important cog in our future adventures.

Renée answered the phone, *"Hi Renée, this is Carolyn. I saw something on TV last night that made me think of you guys and little Jessica..."* she paused.

Carolyn was a friend from church and also a former registered nurse, who was very familiar with our predicament. *"I think you should check it out,"* she went on with excitement in her voice. *"There was a little boy on the show that sounded like he had the exact same problem as Jessica!"* she breathlessly finished. *"Did you see it?"*

Later that evening when I came home from work, Renée shared the information with me. Apparently there had been a program on one of the Sunday evening investigative news shows the night before. The name of the program was *"DPT, The Roulette of Vaccines."*

I then had a quick flash back, and something kind of started to click in the back of my mind. You know the feeling, like when you are doing a puzzle and holding a few pieces in your hand with the nagging idea that you know where they belong, but where?

I thought of Jessica crying unconsolably on Halloween night, and that terrible Friday afternoon, both in close proximity to her DPT vaccinations. My heart jumped! Could it be possible that the answer had been right in front of us all these years?

I resolved to find out.

Tuesday morning, I went to work early. I wanted to be there so I could plan the day and I couldn't wait to get started. We had to see this program, the DPT revelation! I decided to start with the local affiliate, and if they couldn't help me, I would work up the *'food chain'* to the president of the network or whoever could help. I was a man on a mission, and at last the mystery was starting to unravel. I sensed a breakthrough.

"Hello this is Lisa," said the polite voice on the line. *"May I help you?"*

"Hello this is Jim Walker and I am calling from Idaho..."

I had been making calls for nearly two hours. I had called my way all the way up to the network VP of news in New York. The network executive had listened to my inquiry patiently, as I explained my reasons for calling, and then I repeated my questions for the 10th or 12th time:

"Did he know the broadcast I was looking for?"

"Could he get me a copy?"

"Did he know any way I could access the material?"

Realize of course, this was before cable news and before the internet saturation we have today. In retrospect, it was an archaic way to proceed, but it was all I had at the time and I was absolutely not giving up.

"Well, Mr. Walker, I am in complete sympathy with your plight," he said smoothly, *"but,"* 'Uh oh, here comes the rejection again,' I thought, as he continued. *"We only had broadcast rights*

to the program you are seeking, for one time and one time only," he paused to clear his throat. *"However, I can put you in touch with the lady who authored the program and holds the copyright on it, if you would like to try to get her permission."*

I was at the end of the rainbow. One more phone call to go.

After I explained my situation to Lisa, the investigative reporter who had authored the program, and was very sweet, she not only offered to give me a copy of the exact script, but she also said she would overnight ship it to me.

I hung up the phone with a sigh of relief. One more day.

The next morning the package was waiting on my desk and I ripped it open and began to read. And in my mind, as I read, the pieces of the puzzle began drifting slowly down from the gray twilight into the bright light and magically forming a suddenly clear picture. The villain lay exposed before me and as I read on, my heart quickened.

At our neuro clinic check-up with Dr. Burton a few days later, at the end of Jessica's examination, Renée suddenly sat upright and looked him straight in the eye. I could tell by the look on her face, that she had something serious to say.

She carefully posed the possible DPT connection to him, and ended by saying, *"Do you think that could be Jessica's problem?"*

It was a simple question, but with years of medical, emotional, physical and spiritual searching behind it.

After all these long years, it had boiled down to just one question. Renée sat back and waited expectantly.

Dr. Burton sat there silently rubbing his chin and looking a little comical. With his fuzzy hair and unique poses, he reminded me of someone I had seen before. 'Gyro Gearloose,' I concluded, you know, the wacky but brilliant inventor cousin of Donald Duck. Yeah that was it... 'Gyro Gearloose.'

"*Yes,*" he abruptly said, interrupting my thoughts, and now looking more like a wise old wizard. "*Yes, I think that is a definite possibility.*"

To our amazement, he continued, "*...in fact, there is a similar case in Twin Falls, that I have been called on as an expert to offer testimony.*"

Nodding his head he finished, "*Yes! It is worth checking into.*"

I looked at Renée and she was smiling.

Growing Up with JESSICA

The Awakening...

1980's

...the Best Christmas Ever!

Chapter 15

The awakening... the best Christmas ever.

There was a loud muffled banging at the door. Thump! Thump! Thump! Like the sound of someone wearing heavy gloves. I was wrapping presents on the kitchen table. Jessica was laying in the living room on some warm blankets, a safe distance from the softly burning fire, where she could see the twinkling of the Christmas tree lights.

It was the last Sunday before Christmas.

That day had dawned crystal clear and was a welcome break from the record snows of the last week. As the day progressed, it had more and more of a Christmas card look and feel. A bright and shiny, sparkly, drippy day. Icicles were forming on the eve's of our house and the snow softened everything, and by contrast made the sky look incredibly blue. It was a diamond of a day but the real beauty was yet to come.

I opened the door, and there stood two of my neighbors. In the background I could hear the staccato '*bruup... burrp*' of a heavy tractor somewhere near. The snow had made our side streets, including the one in front of our house, a quagmire.

Leaving and arriving was a daily adventure and someone usually needed a little help to get away from the curb and underway. Earlier, Renée and the kids had barely been able to pull away to go shopping.

My neighbors had a proposal. Would I be willing to join everyone else on the block and chip in $20 for gas? My neighbor Ed would then use his backloader to scoop all of the snow off of our street and we could have some relief.

The main roads were plowed and sanded regularly by the city crews but due to the immensity of the snow, all side streets were a '*no man's land.*' Thinking about Renée slipping and sliding that very morning, I quickly agreed.

I turned to head back into the kitchen... hmmm... was it my imagination or had Jessica shifted her position? Naaah! She couldn't have moved, I thought, as I went back to my wrapping, humming '*White Christmas*' in time with the stereo. I was so sure, because Jessica was in what we now call her '*pet rock*' stage. You know. You could put her down and that's exactly where she would be anytime later.

It has been said, '*...the greatest marksman in the world can't hit the bulls-eye if he can't see the target.*' When it comes to seizure control you could add, '*...and doesn't have exactly the right arrow to shoot!*' It is an inexact science to say the least.

One of our neurologists once described the problem like this: "*Imagine all of the telephone systems in the entire world, all of the wires, relays, switches and components that are required, and then multiply that times 100 billion, and that is just an inkling of the complexity and sophistication of the human brain and it's nervous system. And that, Mr. and Mrs.Walker, is what we are up against.*"

At that point in time, we had tried Jessica on just about all of the seizure control medications available. With names like...

phenobarbital, tegretal, clonopin, and don't forget steroids. Yet still, her seizures continued at the same pace, frequency, duration and intensity. We could see very little change.

All of these things, as I am sure you are aware, have 'side effects' and in some cases, it is like trying to tune a Stradivarius violin with a sledge hammer. What you are doing has an effect on the sound but there are rather 'unpleasant' side effects.

Jessica did tolerate things quite well, but each thing we tried subdued her activity more and more. In addition to that, just the stunning effect of the seizures themselves, kind of took her phone off the hook. Thus she sank deeper and deeper into what we now affectionately refer to as her 'pet rock' stage... she was immobilized and kind of subdued in general.

When Jessica was about five years old, we reached what the affable Dr. Burton called "An evolution of decision." We decided that since we weren't seeing any results of the kind we were looking for, maybe we should start dropping the medications, slowly one at a time, and see if Jessica would 'emerge from the fog,' is the way I posed it to the good doctor. He agreed enthusiastically.

Dr. Burton had put us in charge of Jessica's medication. He explained that we were the world's leading experts on her behavior. That if she batted her eyelashes wrong we would notice it, where he only saw her every three months or so.

We shared this arrangement with Renée's sister-in-law Joyce, who in turn shared it with her family doctor who went ballistic when he heard it. He gave her a profanity-laced lecture, ending with the comment, "*Who gave them the PHD in pharmacy and seizure control?*" he demanded.

Joyce was shaken and in near tears when she called us later and shared her experience at the doctor's office. We were a little taken back because of her doctor's vociferous reaction, and thought maybe we had made some kind of error in judgement.

When we shared all of this with Dr. Burton, his reaction was hilarious. He raised himself up to his full height, placed his hand thoughtfully on his chin and with his best mad scientist impression said, "*You tell the good 'docktor' that I gave you the PHD, and have 'heem' call me, if he has any 'qvestshuns!'*" We all had a good laugh at that one.

Finishing my wrapping and hearing the scraping, scooping... braat... zoom... bratt of Ed's tractor, I decided to step out in the warming but crisp afternoon and check his progress. On the way to the front door I glanced at Jessica and froze... hmmm... wasn't she on her back the last time I had checked on her just fifteen minutes ago? Now she was just laying there quietly on her stomach, staring at the twinkling lights on the tree.

Shrugging the thought off, I opened the door and stepped out into the blinding winter afternoon brightness.

The sun was full on the front of the house and in combination with the white snow cover made a very shiny scene. Blinking, I stepped out and shut the door behind me to protect Jessica from the draft.

Ed was just finishing up and had done a marvelous job with the street. Combined with the warming effect of the now exposed black asphalt, the wisps of snow he left behind were melting fast. Our street was now an island of summer in a sea of winter.

Headed home, Ed gave me a friendly wave as he drove by. Since we couldn't speak over the tractor, I simply waved back and gave him a *'thumbs up'* for a job well done.

I stood there admiring the scene. What a perfectly wonderful, beautiful, sparkly pre-Christmas day this was. Very breathtaking I thought, as I turned to go back in the house.

As I opened the door, I looked full into the face of Jessica as she pushed herself up into a sitting position. Propping herself upright with one arm, she glanced quickly around the room and back at her stunned father.

Jessica had awakened! Her eyes had a certain sparkle. A kind of *'look at me Dad,'* expression was on her face.

My eyes began to blur as I thought out loud, *"This is going to be the best Christmas ever!"*

Growing Up with JESSICA

The Photographer...

1984

from Afar...
a Smile.

Growing Up with JESSICA

Chapter 16

The photographer from afar... a smile.

"*Mr. Walker,*" said the eager young voice on the phone. "*I am working on a story about how you and your neighbors banded together and removed the snow from your street and uh... I was wondering if you would be willing to be interviewed. You know, for the article?*" she finished, sounding hopeful.

I turned this new information over in my mind. Was this for real? "*Are you kidding me? Is this a joke?*" I finally said.

"*I'm sorry Mr. Walker. I am calling from the Idaho Statesman newsroom,*" she said, sounding embarrassed, "*I am an assistant reporter on staff, and yes, I really am working on this story for publication.*"

How odd I thought, that anyone out there would be interested in what seemed like a perfectly logical and mundane thing to do... hmmm.

"*Well okay,*" I said. "*Sure.*"

I was feeling rather amused at the whole idea. This must be that '*15 minutes of fame*' I keep hearing about. Some '*expert*' has said that everyone in their lifetime gets their fifteen minutes of fame in the public eye, and I guess I was going to be famous for snow removal! '*How amazing!*' I thought.

And so, I did the interview.

During that same time, Jessica had continued to respond and become much more engaged in her daily life. Sometimes it took the form of protesting angrily and hollering and showing a little temper. On New Years day, She sat up unsupported. Clasping her hands in front of her, and much to our delight, she sat bolt upright, once again looking rather pleased with herself.

I am not really sure how the word got around. Maybe it was from our therapist or our nutritionist, but one of the things that Jessica would do from the very beginning was eat well. Therefore we filled her full of every good thing we could, supplementing her pureed diet with vitamins and supplements, and she responded very well. We had her drink from a bottle with a heavy rubber nipple to improve the muscle tone in her lips. We also followed special procedures with her spoon feeding, to train her tongue, to trying to pro-actively control, the always present choking hazard.

Jessica was the model patient and word of her success eventually got around and this culminated in an interesting series of events which once again involved our daily newspaper. It seems we hadn't completely used up our *'15 minutes of fame'* after all.

"*Mr. Walker,*" the young man nervously began, "*My name is Arnold Gold. I am a photography intern for the Idaho Statesman.*" I thought, '*Holy cow! They are coming back to take pictures of our street,*' but that was months ago, and the snow was long gone.

The promised story about our street snow removal had, in fact, been published as a potential model for dealing with '*local snow removal crises*' in the future. I was even quoted in the article.

114

"It just seemed like the right thing to do, said Jim Walker, of North 30th Street." Oh brother, we all got a big laugh over the 'fame' we had achieved.

It had actually seemed a little silly to me at the time.

"I am calling about your little girl, Jessica." I snapped back to attention. *"I have been assigned to do a human interest photo and short story about her progress. I am a photojournalist,"* he finished, by way of explanation. I was speechless.

Arnold Gold stood shyly on the front steps, as I answered the door a few days later. He had recently graduated from Syracuse University in New York state, and applied for an internship at our paper in Boise, Idaho. He had come in second, the first place guy came, and for some reason didn't want to stay, and so Arnold had landed the job.

He was a very polite and intelligent young guy, I thought, as he gently probed us about Jessica, while fidgeting absentmindedly with his camera bag. He finished up by asking permission to see her and perhaps shoot a few test shots. We said sure and he reached in his bag for his camera and began fiddling with the settings as Renée went to get little Jessica.

In his mind, Arnold was thinking, *'This is a story with a lot of potential.*, as he adjusted his camera, *'This family has something to tell.'*

Arnold was sitting on the wing back chair in the corner of the living room, a vantage point he had gravitated to with the adroit lighting instincts of a photographic artist, placing himself in perfect position to take advantage of the gentle afternoon sun, now streaming in the window.

Renée entered the room with Jessica, as I spread out a large colorful comforter on the carpet in front of an eager Arnold Gold. It was his first assignment, and he was ready.

Jessica was placed on her back at a right angle to the now ready camera. She looked pleasantly around at Arnold and broke into her *first ever smile*. With her dimples showing and her eyes sparkling, as she made eye contact with the lens. *"Click,"* went the camera, as we watched in amazement! After all of these years, Jessica was smiling! She was really smiling with glee at this photographer who had traveled so far to take her picture.

The whole scene was a very precious moment. And it was now recorded on film through this interesting chain of events.

A few days later, the picture of *'smiling Jessica'* was published in full color in the newspaper... a rarity in those days. It was so well received, that Arnold asked our permission to do a follow up assignment, and a more in-depth story.

After witnessing Jessica's reaction to their first meeting, we of course gave him permission. Just as we had anticipated, he carried out the assignment, with tenderness and empathy. He spent a lot of time with us that Spring, and when he wrote the story, it was published as a two-page spread, full of touching photography. It was entitled, *'Jessica, the Blessed One'.*

Arnold did an absolutely marvelous job, and even when read today, it is a heartfelt and moving story. The spread received a national award from the *National Press Photographers Association* (NPPA) in 1984.

A pretty big honor for a job well done.

Just before the story ran, Arnold Gold dropped by our house. He seemed nervous, and had something on his mind. As he tried to make polite small talk, suddenly Renée said, *"You're leaving us, aren't you?"*

"Yes," he said quietly. *" I am leaving tomorrow."*

It was a sad day, because we had grown quite fond of him and his sensitive way of doing his work in the midst of our family. So we went out for ice cream together, and then he zoomed out of our life. For a few years after he returned to the East, we heard from him, as he moved on to a successful career as a photojournalist.

When I began to write this story, I looked at the clippings and photos from our time with Arnold and I couldn't help but wonder where he was and what he was doing. So, I sat down in front of my computer, logged onto the internet, and started searching.

I typed in several different combinations without any luck. Finally, I typed, *'photography/arnold gold.'* I pressed return and bingo, there was his web site! I sent him a quick email.

Arnold responded almost immediately. He was curious and amazed how I had found him, since his web site had been up *less than a week!* Just another interesting coincidence.

He remembered us of course, and commented that he had fond

memories of our time together. He is now married and has a
little girl of his own. He was humbled and touched by the
interest I had in telling about his time with us, in my book.

I asked him for his recollections of that time and he said,
*"Looking back, I feel like you were at a point where you
wanted or needed to share your story, and I happened along
at that point."* he went on to say, *"I know now, as I knew
then, that those were telling moments."*

After I sent him a copy of the manuscript to read, he
thoughtfully responded, *"As I have a daughter now, I
understand more intimately, the vulnerability and joy in their
being, and so, Jessica's story touches me on a different level. I
also understand the immense responsibility of being a parent.
It's joyful, it's aggravating and I always feel like we are laying
the groundwork for the future."*

We will never forget our time together with Arnold Gold, and
the day of Jessica's first smile. A very precious memory.

Just another mysterious and wonderful chain of events that
always seem to surround little Jessica's life.

Unexpected
Help...

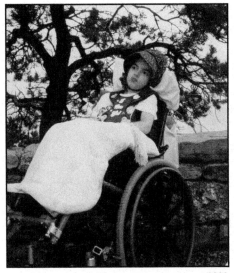

1992

...the Vaccine
Injury Act.

Growing Up with JESSICA

Chapter 17

Unexpected help... the Vaccine Injury Act.

I recently heard a joke about a lady who was praying to God to help her win the lottery, to solve her financial problems. Each week she would plead with Him to let her win, but nothing happened. This went on, week after week, while she slowly lost everything. She lost her furniture, she lost her car, her house was in foreclosure, and so on.

Finally in utter dismay, unable to hide her bitter disappointment, she cried out, "*Please tell me God, why have you forsaken me?*" Suddenly the heavens parted and a bright light beamed down on her, and the voice of God answered, "*Please help me out here lady, and go buy a ticket!*"

I really don't think that God condones gambling but I can relate to that funny story, because I think it underscores the idea that to solve our problems we have to be paying attention, and ready to do our part .

I am thankful that Renée was paying attention one day in the summer of 1989.

She was looking at our mail that day, when she noticed a small article in a Health Department newsletter we receive monthly. It was entitled, '*The Vaccine Injury Act of 1986*.' I had glanced at it earlier, but I hadn't taken the time to read it. She did.

"*Look at this,*" she said excitedly, "*...there is some kind of a law that helps families who have a child that has been injured by a* *vaccination. Wouldn't that be us?"* she said. I must admit, I was pretty skeptical, but I picked it up and began to read.

It seems that there had been a case in Twin Falls, Idaho, that had resulted in a class action law suit. In this case, a small boy who received his DPT vaccinations in the Fall of 1978... I sat bolt upright, with my mind racing!

Renée was absolutely correct.

It had been the fall of 1978 when Jessica's problems began, the same as the boy in Twin Falls, and hadn't our neurologist, Dr. Burton, said something about being an expert witness in a case similar to Jessica's in Twin Falls? I concluded it must be the same case mentioned in the article.

There was a contact number for more information, at the end of the article. I decided to check it out.

I picked up the phone and dialed the number. I still have the note I wrote to myself as I waited on the phone that day. I had scribbled on a notepad, *'...Has any child in Idaho ever successfully pursued this 'vaccine Injury claim' procedure?'*

The lady at the Health Department was both informative and encouraging. She explained that all legal fees we encountered would be reimbursed if we could prove our case, even though no one in Idaho had yet filed a claim. *We would be the first.*

I thought to myself, *'What do we have to lose?'*

We decided to go for it.

Because of our exhaustive attempts to find the 'answer' to
Jessica's medical dilemma, we were pretty confident in our
medical conclusions about Jessica's injuries and the cause of them:
her DPT vaccinations. We had moved heaven and earth and
eliminated every other possible or conjectured theory. This would
be the acid test, and if nothing else, it would settle any remaining
doubts, and of course, the financial impact of Jessica's care was
staggering! We needed help.

To say that there is a huge financial impact in raising a
handicapped child would be an understatement. You just deal
with it as best you can. Insurance helps some, hospitals and
doctors will work with you to a point, but the costs are steep,
relentless and never ending. Discouragement is always waiting
around the corner, since a medical crisis can come upon you
suddenly without warning.

Then there are the 'normal' day to day expenses: things like
special food, supplements, personal care items and of course the
daily medications. Jessica has taken expensive medication four
times daily to help control her seizures, from about age four
months. It adds up.

Don't forget the blood tests and other tests to monitor the
medications, and the check-ups and x-rays. Most children like
Jessica, who experience developmental delays, need 'therapy' to
proceed. Everything from physical muscle and bone stimulation
to proper eating techniques. All of this stuff costs money. Lots
and lots of money!

The question of who provides the ongoing daily care is an
important one both personally and financially. You could hire
someone to do it, have your child become a ward of the state,

never an option for us! Or you can work from home so that you can personally provide the care needed in a loving and caring *'family'* frame of reference. No one could love Jessica like we loved her.

We chose the latter option. I left behind the corporate world and my career and began to work from home as much as possible. As I mentioned earlier, I wanted to share the load with Renée more, and let her have some freedom and balance in her life. It just seemed like the right thing to do for us.

Unfortunately, I didn't always provide financially in the way I would have liked. Our kids Jamie and Jon, helped me many times. One summer our son Jon, who was fifteen, voluntarily went off to Alaska to work in a fish processing plant. He shoveled fish guts on what is politely called the *'slime line',* sometimes working double shifts, to send home money to help make our house payments.

So maybe now you can see why the *'Vaccine Injury Act'* caught my attention. It seemed to offer help and hope at a time that we really needed it.

Jessica was about twelve years old at the time, and we knew there were many years of tough sledding ahead.

Our Personal Crusade Begins...

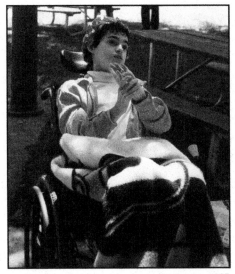

1997

...the Trial.

Chapter 18

Our personal crusade begins... the trial.

After obtaining all of the details about the 'Vaccine Injury Act' we were ready to begin.

Remember, this is before the internet, and there were no handy websites to help us. Today there are many resources available through the 'world wide web', books and guides. Also, I have listed some good ones, in the 'Appendix', as well as a short explanation of the 'Vaccine Injury Act of 1986.'

We knew one thing for sure. We needed to find a lawyer... a good one to help us with the fairly complex procedures and documents we would have to submit. I began to ask around and find someone who would take up our 'crusade.'

I mentioned this to a co-worker who immediately said, "I know just the guy. He goes to my church. His name is Robert Aldridge." I thought, 'another Robert,' remembering Dr. Robert Burton, who working with had been a delight.

It's intriguing to me, that if you look up the meaning of the name 'Robert,' it literally means 'bright fame.' So far it had worked out very well, and so I called and scheduled an appointment.

Another 'Jessica adventure' was about to begin. One that would become very, very important for our future.

We were starting to see some light at the end of our tunnel. The entire 'Vaccine Injury Act' thing, seemed like a fairly straight forward process. *"Surely this can't take very long,"* I had said to Renée confidently... boy was I wrong!

One and a half years later, I sat in the courtroom, nervously fidgeting with my pad and pen, as the Judge began to speak, *"I am going to rule on this case right now without further delay."* My heart was in my throat.

It was May 21, 1991. We had just concluded our case after many, many months of battles and twists and turns, as we struggled against the *United States Department of Justice*, to prove our case.

I had done all of my own research and helped our lawyer prepare our case. We had a unique situation. We had been in the same location and had maintained the continuity of our medical care. All of the doctors and medical records were readily available, and over the years, we had been exhaustive in our elimination of other possible causes.

That was *exactly* the problem. Our case was too good!

And so the legal minds at the *'Justice'* Department decided to make us a *'test case,'* or should I say a *'benchmark,'* if you will. Realize of course, at this time, there had been a very small number of these cases filed and none from our State, and so they knew, if they could find a basis to deny us, it would by legal precedent, set the bar very high for the many cases sure to follow. We were a *pawn* in the greater battle being waged.

So they had turned all of their legal firepower on us to try to destroy our case. To *'shoot us down in flames'* was their goal.

The battle had ebbed and flowed as the months had rolled by.

Initially, they had completely denied our claim by misinterpreting all of the dates. I am not sure if they did that intentionally or accidently, but I do remember staying up all night going over and over the material until I figured out the convoluted way they had twisted the truth. At times, when I felt like throwing in the towel, I would look at Jessica sleeping there, take a deep breath and go on. She was worth fighting for. That night, I resolved in my heart once again, to absolutely never, ever give up.

Now we were facing the moment of truth. We were standing at a critical crossroad in our lives. It was a huge event.

It had been a long exhausting day.

Our lawyer, Robert Aldridge, had turned out to be a real ally and just the 'crusader for justice' we needed. He agreed to take our case 'pro bono.' In other words, he didn't get paid if we lost. He was a tremendously capable and experienced trial lawyer.

We had all testified that day.

Charlotte, who we had thankfully involved in several critical steps along the way, was there, Dr. Burton was there, and many other key witnesses had offered testimony.

I remember when I testified, and the Judge asked me about the Halloween night experience, when Jessica had first been affected. I was describing the moment, when Renée and I had stood by the car and she turned her worried face up to me and said, *"There is something wrong with Jessica!"* When I had tried to say those words, for a few minutes there, I was so overcome with emotion that I couldn't speak. Everything was swimming in front of me. I was back there again, and I could feel the cold night air, the autumn leaves crunching underfoot, and see her breath as she spoke, and it was just too much. The emotion was too strong, as the significance of that moment overwhelmed me. I remember fighting back tears as I struggled to answer.

It was very humbling.

I held my breath, as the Judge began to speak. "*I am ruling in favor of Jessica Walker and her family,*" the judge's booming voice echoed in the hushed room, "*...they are entitled to full compensation.*"

I wrote on my pad that day, just two words... 'WE WON!'

A huge weight had floated off my back. I felt light as a feather! In my mind's eye I could see the beautiful color photo that Arnold Gold had snapped of Jessica that sunny spring day many years before, and Jessica was smiling back at me.

It had been a real '*David versus Goliath*' story, because the giant government entity called '*The Department of Justice*,' had thrown everything at us that they could, but we... had... won!

The Laugh...

1984

...that Shook the Earth.

Growing Up with JESSICA

Chapter 19

The laugh that shook the Earth.

Renée and I went home from court that sunny spring day in May with our hearts full of joy and relief. The battle was over, or so we thought, and we could see nothing but clear sailing ahead. Once again we were naive in our understanding of dealing with the bureaucracy of the *United States Department of Justice.*

I am not a lawyer, but from my experience in dealing with the legal system, I would have to assume, that on their first day at Law School in *'How to be a Lawyer 101'* or something, the very first principle covered must be, *'how to delay and obstruct.'*

Much to our amazement, even though the Judge ruled that day from the bench, and gave them 90 days to settle our claim, the process had dragged on for nearly a year after that point, with practically no end in site.

Finally, in May 1992, at our wits end, we decided to *'go on the warpath'*... so to speak. We jumped into the battle to fight for Jessica, one more time. This time I was determined to seek complete and absolute victory.

I turned to Idaho Senator Larry Craig for help. I sat down and wrote him a long letter detailing our frustrations and the run arounds on top of run arounds we were wading through. I mailed it to his office in Boise and waited.

A week went by and nothing. No phone calls, no letters. And so, I called his administrative assistant, to seek an answer.

Another small miracle happened that day. He was holding my letter in his hands, *when* he answered the phone. "*Yes. He was on it,*" he said, "*and he would get to the bottom of it if he had to move heaven and earth.*"

I had to smile at that comment, but later it got even better.

Larry Craig's assistant called back later and said he and Senator Craig "*Had rattled some cages in Washington D.C.*"...as he put it. He did happen to mention to me the name of the actuarial firm and the representative working on our case. Just a few names, nothing else. I waited a few days, and hearing nothing further, I gritted my teeth and determined to see it through to the end. I decided to take matters into my own hands.

Armed with the name of the company and the person assigned to our case, I started making calls. First, I had to assume that a company large enough to do such work for the government would have offices in the financial hubs of the country. Places like Boston, New York, Baltimore, etc.

"*What city please?*" asked the operator. I hesitated. Hmmm... taking a stab in the dark, I said, "*Baltimore,*" and then the name of the actuarial company... bingo! The phone was ringing and the receptionist answered, "*Good Morning, this is Structured Financial Services. How may I help you?*" I held my breath, "*Yes, may I speak with Robert Edwards please?*" I said, smiling at the thought. There was that name again.

Would he be my next '*bright fame*.' This was starting to get a little amazing, but I didn't know the half of it. "*I am sorry,*" she began, '*Oops, I must have blown it,*' I thought, "*...but Robert is*

*working in Alexandria, Virginia for a few days. Would you
like that number?"*

Would I? Would I? I could hardly stand it!

"Why, yes if it's no trouble," I said, trying to sound calm and
professional and yet contain my excitement. But wait, it gets
much better!

I sat there looking at the number written in front of me. I was
thinking, *'Is this the end of the road, or just another
beginning?'* I decided to press on and began to dial.

"Rinnnng... rinnnng!" I let it ring over and over. No answer. I
started to hang up and then I heard a voice, *"Hello... hello?"* the
voice said, sounding slightly out of breath. *"This is Robert!"*

*"Mr. Edwards, this is Jim Walker from Boise, Idaho and I am
calling on behalf of my little girl Jessica."* I took a deep breath
and forged ahead. *"Jessica was injured by her DPT
vaccinations and is entitled to compensation under the Vaccine
Injury Act. It has been almost a year and we have not been
compensated,"* I said rather doggedly, *"...and I am told that you
are the person that is holding things up!"* On the other end of
the line, there was a dead silence.

After what seemed like an eternity, he began to speak.

*"Mr. Walker, I apologize to you and your little girl. I am not
trying to dodge my responsibility, but I have been trying for six
months to get the information from the Justice Department
representatives to work on your case ..."* Hmmm, I thought,
that sounded familiar, *"...but, things are moving now,"* he said.

"Let me explain!"

I listened with great interest to his description of the recent amazing sequence of events. Apparently Senator Craig had called the *Chief of the Justice Department*, to expedite our case. When Craig was told that the Chief was leaving on vacation in the morning and had gone home early that day, the good Senator called him at home that evening!

We don't know the content of their conversation, but it was sufficient to motivate the Chief to change his plans and go into his office the next day and start the wheels turning.

You could say he was inspired.

Magically, the input that Robert Edwards needed was available and had a major rush stamped on it. Robert had been in Richmond that day testifying before a Grand Jury, as an expert witness under subpoena. They went into the Grand Jury room, removed him, handed him the files, and gave him his marching orders, *"Finish up and forward the Jessica E. Walker, Vaccine Injury case, now, without delay. Expedite it!"* Robert chuckled as he related this to me. *"Apparently someone had lit a major fire under their tail feathers!"* We both laughed.

Robert had left as soon as the Grand Jury adjourned for the day, and driven back to Alexandria. He worked until 4 a.m. finishing Jessica's case. He had then taken it down to the express mail office and mailed it, drove home, showered and shaved, grabbed a quick bite to eat and rushed back to his office. As he entered, the phone was ringing off of the hook, and he had rushed to answer it gasping and out of breath...

...and it was ME calling!

Another big coincidence or a small miracle.

We both had a good laugh. In spite of the conditions that we met under, I liked him. He was honest and sincere and he offered to send me copies of everything, which he did and they have been very helpful even up to this very day.

Robert was a non-government private contractor, and after a short discussion about the perils and frustrations of working with a bureaucracy, we said our goodbyes on cordial terms.

I thought, whew! Now things will be okay. I was wrong again!

Weeks went by, and although I did get the materials Robert Edwards had promised me, nothing else happened. I tracked our case down again in the bowels of the bureaucracy, finally speaking with the head of the department responsible for the the most recent delay.

The conversation went something like this.

I said, *"Look, I don't want to come to Washington D.C. and hold a news conference in your lobby, but, I WILL if you don't expedite this today!"*

Gritting my teeth, I went on, *"Today is Wednesday and you have until Friday, or I promise you, I WILL be coming to Washington to speak with you or your boss or your boss's boss! Have you got that?"*

It worked! On Friday, everything was done. It had been a long and exhausting grind, but, the log jam was broken.

We were able to purchase a new handicapped equipped van, and we decided to take a long trip to unwind and celebrate. So Renée, Jessica and I packed up and headed out, leaving our kids, Jamie and Jon in charge of everything at home. We went East.

At that time, I was the Director of the *All American Soap Box Derby* in Boise, and I needed to haul the cars to Akron for the World Championships. Then it was on to Watkins Glen, New York, to find Renée's long lost relatives. After that, to the Florida panhandle to visit my sister who was in poor health, and also to rendezvous with my Mom, Jamie and Jon, for a surprise *'Birthday Party'* for Renée and Jessica (Renée had no idea!) on August 25th.

On the drive home, another precious moment came our way.

We had been traveling around the Grand Canyon as we headed for home, taking the scenic route through Utah's rugged and unique *Zion National Park.*

As we drove along in the gathering sunset, we hesitated at the entrance to the lodge grounds and camping area. Should we pull in and spend the night or push on?

As Renée steered the van around the winding road perched on a hill side, I looked at Jessica. She looked happy and content, looking quietly out at the scenery. *"Let's keep going,"* I said. *"There's a 'rest stop' when we get to the freeway and we can spend the night there."*

At the rest stop, we made our bed in the van, and placed Jessica between us. As we lay there I just impulsively reached out and stroked her chin. As she turned to look at me, she began to giggle and then *laugh out loud!* A beautiful, musical, gurgling laugh, like the sound of a little brook happily rushing along. It was infectious and we both laughed with her, and the sound of a thousand angels couldn't have been any sweeter!

It was the first time we had heard her laugh like that and we didn't want it to stop. Later as I dozed off, I could still hear it in my head. I remembered the first time I had ever heard her tiny heartbeat and I realized how very, very much I loved this precious little girl, now sleeping next to me, who had turned our world upside down!

I woke up suddenly with a start... something was wrong!

The van was swaying violently in every direction at once, it seemed! I thought of the trailer we were pulling, full of *Soap Box Derby* cars, tools and equipment. Someone must be breaking into the trailer, I sleepily concluded. I balanced myself in the rocking van and looked out the back window. I saw nothing... nothing at all. Just the dimly lit rest stop full of loaded semis and other weary travelers. Then slowly, the shaking stopped, and an eery quiet settled in.

I woke Renée. "*Whaaat was that?*" I shouted. "*What was what?*" she said groggily.

Had I imagined it, I wondered? No! That was real. I didn't know what had happened, but the van had been shaking hard. At the same time, I was wondering why Renée, usually a light sleeper, hadn't noticed? Then the roaring started, as the dozen or so 18 wheelers parked around us, began to roar to life and lumber away in the darkness. What was going on? Well, I didn't know, but if they were leaving... we were leaving! I looked at the clock, as I started the van. It was 3:45 am.

As we drove on to Salt Lake City, I heard the report on the radio. Apparently there had been a big earthquake, and the epi-center was located just a few miles from where we had been sleeping. So that was it!

The next day it was big news! A photo on the front cover of the Salt Lake paper grabbed my attention. There was a large picture of the very road we had been on just a few hours before the earthquake hit. It was *buried* under 30 feet of rock and dirt!

'*Whoa,*' I thought, '*...that was close!*'

We could have easily been buried in that landslide.

Then I thought of Jessica's big belly laugh the night before. When I showed the picture to Renée, I said, "*Jessica laughs out loud... and the earth shakes!*"

As I ran things through my mind that morning, I had to wonder to myself...

'*Just exactly what had she been laughing about?*'

An Amazing Dream...

1990's

...a Taste of the Future.

Chapter 20

An amazing dream... a taste of the future.

Ron reached out cautiously to his sleeping daughter Kacey, and wondered about her breathing. It seemed non-existent and he couldn't see any movement. None. Feeling slightly alarmed, he shook her gently and then harder.

She awoke with a start!

"Thanks, daddy, for waking me up," Kacey, said groggily. *"I was having a bad dream. Well, not really a bad dream, but..."* she hesitated.

We all know of at least a few things that we have in common. For instance, a body, a mind and a spirit or soul or as the Bible says *"...heart, mind and soul..."* Of course we do.

What about a child like Jessica? What does she have, you might ask, or at least think? She is compromised. You know, 'handicapped,' so, isn't she just an empty shell?

I will admit, that these questions are faced at some point, by every parent who finds themselves in our position. Especially in our sometimes prevalent 'throw-away' society.

We have all been exposed to those who say, *"Don't like that thing, just throw it away."* or *"Are those older relatives a pain in the neck? Just, cast them off!"* *"Don't want that unborn baby? Just throw its life away."* And, on and on.

So, you can imagine the 'looks' and the 'comments' that come our way. Comments like, *"We could easily terminate this pregnancy,"* or *"You two deserve your time together, without this burden,"* or *"We could have her institutionalized. You know, so you could be free!"*

Sometimes the odd looks we get, say it all.

People who don't know her, look at Jessica. She is a rather petite little girl who cannot speak or sing, walk, run or jump or play. She can't stand or feed herself or scratch her curly, black hair covered head but they can't see her mind or her soul, and believe me, they are there. She is temporarily trapped in a tough physical condition, but, there is much more to her than meets the eye.

I sometimes watch Jessica as she is sleeping and I watch her dreaming. I know she is dreaming, because I can see her eyes moving under her eyelids, and some slight movements in her extremities. The expression on her face will change. Sometimes a dimpled smile, once in a while she will actually wake up smiling happily, and looking very pleased. I marvel at this very sweet activity and I pause as I wonder...

'Just exactly what... is she dreaming about?'

Kacey went on, *"I was somewhere above the room looking down, and then I noticed a bright light, and someone was walking towards me,"* she said, shaking off the effects of her sleep medication, *"...and then, I thought I recognized the person walking out of the light..."* she paused again.

Renée and I look forward to the day when we will behold the

completely restored Jessica. Sometimes we get a taste, just a taste, of what that will be like. A taste of the future. The dream that Kacey had that day is a part of that future promise.

Kacey took a breath and continued, *"...and as I looked, and the person walking got closer, I could see that... that it was Jessica!"* she blurted out. *"She reached down and took my hand and said, 'Kacey, Jesus loves you. You have cancer, but you are going to be all right!' "*

Renée's brother Ron's daughter Kacey, had gone into the out patient surgery that day for what was supposed to be a one hour surgery to remove a cyst. Her operation lasted over 4 hours because the doctors had discovered an unidentified mass and had taken samples for a biopsy.

The test results were to come in a few days.

Ron, and his wife Joyce, had taken their little daughter home that day, to recover from the grueling procedure. Kacey had fallen into a deep sleep from which Ron had aroused her and then she had begun to share her amazing dream.

There was more.

Jessica had continued, *"Tell my mom and dad that I love them, and that I will be okay!"* and then Kacey was awakened and the dream had ended.

Yes, Kacey did turn out to have a very serious form of cancer with a very high mortality rate that was confirmed when her biopsy was completed a few days later. And yes, she did survive, and survives to this day.

When Renée and I first heard about this dream, we were amazed, and it touched our hearts. Jessica had said she loved us, in a very dramatic way, and was apparently trying to send us some kind of a message. *"I will be okay,"* she had said to Kacey. *"I will be okay."*

Well, of course she would. After all, weren't we taking very careful care of her? However, at that point in time, we had no idea what was waiting around the bend for us.

We had missed her bigger point.

Jessica's message wasn't a confirmation of what we knew. It was a word of warning and encouragement concerning the future.

"I will be okay." she had said, *"I WILL be okay."* At the time, the significance of her statement went right over our heads.

But a day was fast approaching when those four little words would be the most precious words in our memory.

During that traumatic experience, yet in the future, we would cling tenaciously to Jessica's promise to us, spoken to Kacey that day, many months earlier in her amazing dream!

A Major Surgery...

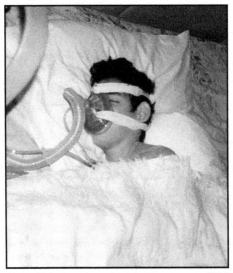

1996

...the Confirmation of Love.

Chapter 21

A major surgery... the confirmation of love.

I walked slowly up the four flights of stairs, on my way to the pediatric critical care ward.

Entering the shiny double doors, I paused to scrub up with disinfectant at the sink, and then made my way to the back corner room that had been Jessica's home for the last 10 days. The curtain door was closed. There must be something going on I thought, as I quickened my pace.

Quietly and slowly opening the door, I looked expectantly towards Jessica's bed. Dr. Forester, stethoscope to her ears, looked up and smiled absentmindedly as she leaned over Jessica, carefully listening to her heart. Just a routine check-up I thought with relief, as the monitoring equipment attached to Jessica beeped rapidly in the background.

I looked at Jessica lying there, with tubes and wires coming out all over her body, and a respirator covering her face and nose to help her breathe. Our eyes met.

"*Hi Jessica!*" I said cheerfully. "*How's my girl?*" As I reached out, and took her small delicate fingers in my hand, a thought came rushing back from the past, "*...look, she has the hands of a pianist. She's going to grow up to be a great concert pianist!*"

"*That's remarkable... just remarkable!*" said Doctor Forester, interrupting my thoughts, as the insistent beeping rapidly declined, followed by a plummeting of Jessica's vital sign numbers. I looked up and watched them tracing themselves in green, on the monitor. *"Jessica sure knows her daddy! That really is remarkable!"* the doctor finished.

Surprised at her comments, I looked at Dr. Forester. She was looking at me in amazement, a broad smile on her youthful face.

We had met Dr. Forester as a part of the brilliant surgical team, that had operated on Jessica. Her speciality is *'Pediatric Cardiology.'* That's a *'heart doctor for little kids.'* We liked her almost immediately and the tender way that she interacted with Jessica. She was a young, but excellent doctor, now doing follow up in the hospital.

Jessica was recovering from major surgery.

One of the physical ailments that comes with the territory, when you have a developmentally delayed child, is something called *'scoliosis'* of the spine. It occurs, because the child, as they are growing up, may not be able to stand and walk and maintain even muscular pressure up and down their spine. The muscles attached to the spine, develop with a lack of balance in their strength, or the amount of pull they exert. This uneven pull can twist and curve the spine and results in the medical condition I refer to... *'scoliosis.'*

Scoliosis is almost always inevitable with a child like Jessica, and your goal through interventional therapy is to delay the corrective surgery that will be needed, for as long as possible.

For instance, it is best to get beyond the teenage *'growth years,'* to avoid needing multiple surgeries.

The surgery I am describing here is a '*major*' surgery. Add in the fact that you are dealing with a fragile health status in Jessica's case, and I think you can see it is dangerous.

So why did we decide to go ahead with this major surgery? Why were we putting little Jessica's life at such risk by putting her through all of this, you may ask?

Well, the answer to those questions is that the side effects of not treating it can be fatal, putting undue pressure on the heart and other critical organs. So, even though we had hoped to avoid the surgery, it became eventually apparent, that to extend Jessica's life span we had to go ahead with it. So, we located the best surgical team we could find, set the date, and moved on to another '*adventure*' with Jessica.

We had tried to prepare Jessica for her hospital trip, and since we couldn't sit down with her and explain things, we had to look for other ways to ease the shock. There were so many things we wanted to tell her, like what would happen and why all this was necessary, but it just wasn't possible. I remember, at the time it was such a heartache as the date for her surgery approached.

Three more days. Two more days. Today's the day.

So we did everything we could to help her feel at ease with the hospital surroundings. We took her down there for a few visits, where the *Critical Infant Care Unit* (CICU) nurses actually let us go and sit in the room where she would be.

We played beautiful, uplifting, instrumental music and hymns for her constantly. Then we got permission to place a stereo by her bedside, so that we could play the same CDs for her after her surgery and during her hospitalization and recovery.

She had a bright and cheery room, and with the music constantly playing, it became a calm little island of serenity in the life and death storms of the critical care unit. Many of the nurses would seek it out on their breaks and they came to love the atmosphere in Jessica's room.

The surgery had been an all day affair, involving two different operations. One from the front and one from the back. The orthopedic surgeon had called us periodically during the surgery, giving us updates: *"She is doing very well," "Everything is going as planned,"* was the report. Her surgery finished. She had been taken through recovery and on in to the children's critical care unit. The entire hospital trip was supposed to be three or four days, and five at the max. We were now on our tenth day, with no end in sight.

The problem? Three unsuccessful attempts to 'wean' Jessica off the 'respirator,' the machine that was keeping her breathing steadily and feeding her a higher level of oxygen. It was a critical step in her recovery, that had ended in failure each time, with Jessica gasping for breath and her heart and respiration rate, racing wildly. Failure after failure after failure.

Her progress had stalled.

"I have an idea Mr. Walker," Dr. Forester said, with sudden inspiration. *"I think it just might work."* the doctor continued, still smiling. *"Yes, I think it could work!"*

From the time I had first met Jessica, and she reached out to me that day in the hospital and grabbed my finger so tightly, we had experienced a kind of special bond. It was as if she were saying with her tight little hand...

"Hold me daddy... hold me tight!"

Every day since, I have hugged and kissed her and treated her tenderly. Sometimes just sitting on the floor and softly scratching and rubbing her little head as she relaxes and drifts off to dreamland. Sometimes when Jessica was ill or having trouble sleeping, Renée and I would nestle her down between us in bed, and rub her feet or stroke her forehead to comfort her, treasuring the closeness of the experience.

As she grew up, more and more apparently disabled, we didn't stop the hugs. We just held her all the tighter, and she would relax and coo and look happy and safe in our arms.

As I have said many times, if love would cure her, she would be the healthiest kid on the planet. Her brother and sister have also showered her with affection over the years.

Jessica is a very special child to us.

We have always treated her with dignity and respect. She is not unworthy of our attention because she is 'handicapped.' We have always assumed that she was able to understand us and accept our affection and care, even though she was unable to verbalize it. We have always spoken to her as a person and did every thing that we could to communicate our love to her.

"Mr. Walker, are you... uh... squeamish at all?" said Dr. Forester eagerly, as I wondered what she was getting at.

"Do you think you would be able to assist us in removing Jessica's respirator?" as she finished, watching me closely.

I flashed back over the last eighteen years of Jessica's life.

The endless tests. The CT Scans. Magnetic Resonance Imaging scans. Not to mention the poking of her tiny arms with needles. The relentless drawing of blood for analysis and the late nights in the emergency room, and more shots and blood and bandages. Jessica lying in the gaping mouth of the CAT Scan machine in her little pink dress, with the red cross hairs focused on her tiny forehead. I ended the emotional kaleidoscope on the heart stopping image of her sitting up on the gurney ten days before, and looking back innocently at her shaking parents, as she passed through the big metal swinging doors on her way into surgery.

And then, I looked at Jessica lying there on the hospital bed in front of me, all hooked up like some kind of an experiment gone wrong, staring intently up at me. I was feeling the steady pressure of her warm little grip on my hand.

'Squeamish?' I had to smile at that question.

In the background, the sound of the monitoring equipment had dropped to a mere whisper. *"YES! I will do it, doctor. Anything, you want."* I said firmly, *"Yes, anything!"*

It had slowly begun to sink in, that there before me, was the undeniable *'scientific proof,'* if you will. The proof of Jessica's awareness and understanding and love. The calming effect that my words and touch had on her vital signs, told me she was *'in there'* and the *'lights'* were on. She knew me and responded to me, and my voice and presence and my touch had comforted her in a *"...remarkable way,"* as the doctor had put it. I knew that we would be successful with the procedure this time. Besides, hadn't Jessica told us, *"I WILL be okay? Tell my Mom and Dad that I WILL be okay!"* It was an amazing moment, as once again, I was comforted by those words.

I was right, the doctor was right, and Jessica was right. The very next day we successfully removed her respirator and she began to grow stronger and mend. Jessica was going to be, *"...okay!"* and we counted another wonderful blessing.

Three weeks earlier, after Jessica's surgery, as we sat in the hospital, waiting for our first peek at her, waiting for the nurse to summon us to Jessica's room, the memory of Jessica's words in her cousin Kacey's dream months before, had all flooded into my mind. I had understood for the first time, the amazing dream and what Jessica had said so clearly, *"Tell my mom and dad that I love them and... I WILL be okay!"*

"Mr. and Mrs. Walker," said the CICU nurse, *"You can see her now."* I had looked at Renée on that first day of Jessica's surgery and she was pale and trembling.

"Don't worry," I said softly as I looked into her eyes, *"Jessica, will be okay. Remember what she said in Kacey's dream."*

Renée's eyes had slowly widened and the color had returned to her face. *"Yes,"* she said, breathing a sigh of relief, *"Yes, I remember,"* As she whispered in my ear, and kissed me tenderly on the cheek, *"I do remember!"*

Twenty-one days after Jessica had sat up on the operating room gurney and looked back innocently at us as she passed through the big swinging doors on her way to surgery, while we had both stood there with our hearts in our throats, wanting to run and grab her back and carry her off somewhere safe and secure, with no more blood and no more tears, she came home again.

Safe again, at last she returned home, but this time with the very real confirmation of our mutual love for each other.

Jessica was not an *'empty shell.'* She was a person who could receive and respond to our love for her. She was loving us back.

The bond of love between us was growing stronger than it had ever been.

Hanging in There...

1990

...the Long Haul.

Chapter 22

Hanging in there... the long haul.

In your life, has anyone you loved very, very much, ever died and left you grieving? Imagine, if you will, experiencing that feeling every single day of your life. Now you know what we have felt. I am not telling you this, so you will feel sorry for us, nor am I trying to be overly dramatic. I am just trying to find the words and the illustrations to communicate what it feels like, because in many ways... it is unspeakable. Even now after many years it is painful to relive the memories and the heartbreak through which we have traveled. It was a sometimes barren and forbidding landscape. The daily heartbreak alone, as it accumulates, is enough to destroy you. I have shared the unvarnished truth of our experience.

Of course, I don't know why you are reading this book. Maybe you are just curious. Maybe you have had a similar journey in life. Maybe you are now facing a journey down a sudden road that you never planned to travel. Maybe it is you or your child, or a dear relative, or someone you love, that has entered into this new and perilous, unexpected world. It's going to be a long, long and difficult journey. How can you hang in there?

I do know why I am sharing our story. I want to help others. Maybe you are that one person who will be helped. If sharing our story and how we survived helps you, or someone you know, then I can say, *"Hurray! It was worth the pain of reliving it! "*

In the process of writing this book, I have shared it with many other people. Some of them knew us and some didn't.

Growing Up with JESSICA

Everywhere we go we find someone who has a need and we share our story with them and send them copies of the book in progress and they were touched and comforted and encouraged. We do rejoice in that.

I have received a lot of feedback and suggestions. A number of people were curious as to the depth and breadth of our daily routine in caring for Jessica. Without belaboring the point, but to satisfy your curiosity, here is what we are dealing with daily.

Jessica is a 'total care' situation and cannot do anything to care for herself. We perform all of the routine care such as bathing, combing her hair, trimming her nails. She is still in diapers, so we change her five or six times a day.

On a daily basis, our schedule looks like this:

I arise by 6 am daily and start her breakfast and crush her seizure medication. I add it to applesauce and give it to her, and then change her diapers. Renée then gives her an 'airway clearance' treatment and then feeds her breakfast and washes her up and grooms her. At noon one of us feeds her lunch and her second dose of seizure control medication, and then puts her down for a nap.

At 6 pm I give her a second 'airway clearance' treatment and then I fix her dinner and feed her and give her her third dose of medication. About 11 p.m. she gets her final dose of medication, a diaper change, and is tucked into bed with a kiss.

So there you have it. That is pretty much the routine we have followed every day of her life. It has been a long haul.

Please don't feel sorry for us. That is not necessary. We consider caring for Jessica a privilege and a labor of love. There is nothing quite like feeding her, with one hand on her curly little head, while looking into her eyes, as she eagerly opens her mouth like a sweet little bird, eager to be fed. It is a great time.

The other question that has repeatedly come up, is about our other two children, Jamie and Jon. What has been their reaction and how has all of this changed them?

I have shared a few of my memories with you in these pages. My original idea was to write the first draft of this book, have them read it and then share that. I forgot one thing. Reading the book was as difficult for them, as it was for me to write it. It just broke them down to relive it. I think that gives you an idea of how *'growing up with Jessica'* has impacted them. So I decided to take another approach. I put together a few questions and asked them to respond. Here is their feedback.

Jamie's thoughts about 'growing up' with Jessica:

I was ten when Jessica was born, so at an early age I realized that she was not like other three year olds. It became more obvious to me how really different she was when my parents brought home her first wheel chair. That chair brought in a wave of harsh reality that I would never be able to experience the enjoyment of having a "baby sister" as I had anticipated. There was a huge disappointment and often anger that I was robbed the joys of shopping at the mall or going to a movie with my little sister.

In my late teenage years I began to realize that there may never be a change in Jessica's life, that maybe the change was going to be in the lives that surrounded her and that maybe the healing would be in our family and the people we encountered.

Through the years, it became apparent that Jessica's disability was allowed by God for a greater purpose than I could comprehend. The lives that I saw touched by God through my family and especially my parents, was amazing. It seemed that my parents had an innate ability to really speak to those who were hurting. They were able to share their experience with a certain peace about God's plan for our lives. You could see that amidst this terrible situation they were filled with compassion for others and true joy about their future with Jessica.

Shortly after graduating from high school, around the time of Jessica's ninth birthday, I remember fearing for the first time that my parents may not make it through the struggles. There was a lot of hurt, guilt and bitterness that I could see as they learned to deal with the reality that a decision that ultimately they had made had changed our lives forever.

They had made the decision to give Jessica her immunization with the counsel of our family doctor. They had made the decision based on what they believed to be the best for Jessica and society told them it was the right thing to do. Ultimately, they made the decision and as an end result they would be given the opportunity to touch lives forever with their story.

The road seems long at times and there are still difficulties we face but looking back now at our lives with Jessica it is easy to see the blessings experienced as a result of her disability.

My parents have made an amazing and sacrificial decision to keep Jessica at home and care for her every day. We have been committed as a family to surrounding her with love, and felt that the best way to do that was to have her home with us.

I am still amazed at the sacrifices that my parents make and the lives that they touch every day with joy in their heart. I have come to truly believe that the trials we are given, with the right heart and God's intervention, make us so much better in all aspects of life.

Our family has learned so much from this experience, and although there are times that are tough, we have grown so much as individuals. The bond that we share as a family is amazing and it has been a true blessing to experience the changes I have seen in our lives. Personally, my sister, Jessica, has caused me to have so much more empathy for the hurts and struggles that I see people dealing with every day.

Although Jessica can't walk, can't speak a word and needs constant care and attention, she has touched and truly changed more lives than I could count. What a true blessing it has been to have a "baby sister" so loved by God!

Jon's thoughts about life with Jessica:

Having Jessica for a sister has changed me!

It has made me more sympathetic toward people with disabilities and empathetic toward the parents. When I see someone with a disability, I often find myself trying to make eye contact, spark a conversation, ease the awkwardness of the siblings and praise the parents for their commitment. A recent example that comes to mind was when my entire family (yes, Jessica too) went on a cruise celebrating my parents' 40th. anniversary. Before jumping on the ship, we were returning one of the rental cars... in true Walker fashion. We were right on time... about an hour and a half late! (Any of you that have a disabled person in your family... know what I'm talking about.)

In the parking lot, there was a mother and her two daughters. One of them with a striking resemblance to Jessica at that age.

163

Growing Up with JESSICA

I was drawn to them. I remember the connection I had with the sister of this particular individual. She was about fifteen, and although we had never met before, I knew we shared the same road. I tried to encourage her and challenge her never to be embarrassed about the gift she had been given in her little sister. It was a tearful conversation. We visited, introduced Jessica to them, shared stories, laughed and even cried together; it was ordained that we met.

I would like to think Jessica has made me more sensitive and perceptive of people's special and/or unspoken needs, but above all, I have observed the power of Love. I could not have asked for better parents to be that model.

Jon's wife Sara shares about the influence on Jon of growing up with a little sister like Jessica:

I have observed that people always come first with him. The decision between people and projects is never a hard one for him. It's just in him to always care for people first.

This may or may not be because of 'growing up with Jessica,' but I have noticed that he has an unusual ability to be level-headed in a crisis. God has used him many times as he's been the first one to the scene of an accident, or the time he discovered two girls drowning in the ocean and saved their lives. It's interesting how God seems to place him in those situations so frequently. I'm guessing it is because He knows Jon can handle it.

He is very sentimental. He's also more comfortable than most men with showing his emotions. When he's sad or moved by something he doesn't hold back. He's not ashamed to cry. I love that.

How my Family's Love Saved Me.

Well, there is just a little insight into the life-impact on Jamie and Jon, that has come as a result of the experience of having a little sister who is a special and unique little person.

Jamie is a successful self-employed business woman here in Boise. She is married and has a daughter, Emerson Elizabeth.

Jon is the Executive Director of a large Christian Camp in nearby McCall, Idaho. He is married and has three young boys, Elijah James, Jacob Pierce, and Benjamin David Walker.

I can vouch for the love and tenderness and empathy that they all have, because recently I experienced it first hand. The day I was due to finish this book I was hospitalized with acute pneumonia. I was in critical condition, with an especially sneaky, hard to detect, and deadly strain of bacteria that completely blindsided me. Aptly named *'the silent death.'*

I spent eight days in the hospital, and about the first four I was barely hanging on. A grave is six feet deep and I think I checked into the hospital at about the four foot level.

During that entire eight days, my kids and my wife never left me alone. I was in intense pain. I hurt all over. I couldn't sleep and I was exhausted. Jamie or Jon or Renée were there massaging my back, feet and head... sometimes all at once. They fed me and brought me ice chips and encouragement.

I can honestly say that they saved my life with the unselfish love they showered on me. I know it was the difference.

With their love and God's comforting assurance, I recovered. It was an experience I will never forget. It was amazing.

If their unselfish love and empathy had not saved me, you would not be reading this book. Jessica's influence was there.

Earlier I asked the question. *"What would you do when faced with a situation with no easy solution?"* No quick fix. A problem that strikes at your very heart and soul and just won't go away! Your life and everything in it is forever changed.

I explained what we did. We staggered forward.

We are often asked the question in various forms. Sometimes spoken, sometimes implied. *'How do you manage to go on?'* It's a natural question. Well, we have staggered forward and grown stronger. Not because we are super human, super smart, or super saints. It is possible because we have discovered something that is greater than anything else in life.

On page one, I shared how Renée and I had begun our married life together by looking for the answers to life and the meaning of real love, *'unselfish love,'* through our study of the Bible.

We found those answers, and have experienced, rather unwillingly at times, the real fleshed out impact of the definition of true *'unselfish'* or sacrificial love. My recent trip to the hospital is just another example.

We discovered that we each have a soul, and God in his wisdom, has given us an *'Owner's Manual'* called the Bible. *"Greater love has no one than this, that he lay down his life for his friends."* That is the Biblical definition of unselfish or *'agape'* love.

If you practice it... it will change you, because you could say it is the love of God. It is the true nature of God.

We all have to chose on what to build our life. Life is full of
choices, and every choice has a result or a consequence.
That is a principle of life that is inescapable.

In the Bible there is an illustration shared by Jesus Christ in the
book of Matthew, that is an appropriate lesson to consider.

*"Everyone who hears these words of mine and puts them into
practice, is like a wise man who built his house on the rock.*

*The rain came down and the streams rose, and the winds
blew and beat against that house; yet it did not fall,
because it had its foundation on the rock.*

*But everyone who hears these words of mine and
does not put them into practice is like a foolish man
who built his house on sand.*

*The rain came down and the streams rose, and the winds
blew and beat against that house,
and it fell with a great crash."*

Jesus Christ in Matthew 7:24-27 NIV

Our experiences with Jessica have taught us that lesson very
well, and we continue to explore the breadth and depth of God's
seemingly endless and bottomless, love and wisdom, on a daily
basis. It is there for you and everyone.

God is the most important difference in our lives. God is what
has given us the strength and perseverance to not only go on, but
to prosper in our tragedy. We have been able to survive the 'long
haul' and face the future boldly, but not alone.

Growing Up with JESSICA

We have built our house on the 'solid rock' of faith in God, and the storms of life have nearly swamped us, more than once, but we have survived, and grown stronger!

God is the key to our survival and He is how we go on. We have prospered in our pain and Jessica has been the catalyst.

God is how we go on, with our hearts broken.

God is the key to survival in good times and bad.

Your survival and mine... in the 'long haul.'

Growing Up...

1980's

...with Jessica..

Chapter 23

Growing up with Jessica... she fixed us, as we 'grew up' with her.

So there you have it... a peek into Jessica's life, and our lives.

The true story.

Renée and Jamie and Jon and Jessica and I, have been on this exciting adventure in 'Jessica-land' for many, many years now and it has sometimes been a wild ride.

There have been the slow moments of mysterious anticipation, like a roller coaster climbing to the top of a precipice, and then a few giddy, giggly, light moments at the top, before you rush downward into the void with a goosebump popping rush.

You rush right and left, up and down, barreling suddenly around a corner into the dark and out again into the blazing light. It is definitely not boring, if you know what I mean.

I have done my very best for you.

I have tried to give you an honest sample of how we have staggered on, and why and how. How we grew stronger, overcoming despair and *growing up* right along with Jessica.

As I said earlier, I may not know who you are or why you are reading this. However, I do know this. You and I may never pass this way again, and so I have shared the innermost thoughts of my heart with you to hopefully offer you the same hope that I have discovered. I am not ashamed to admit, that many times the tears came as I relived the good times and the bad, along with you.

Our family is not somehow super special. We are just an ordinary family in extraordinary circumstances.

Renée and I have discovered something vitally important. In fact, it is the most important discovery of our lives. It is what I call the *'answers to life.'*

I mentioned before how Renée and I began to study the Bible, looking for answers to questions like, *"Is GOD really out there?"* or *"Was the Bible TRUE?"* or *"What was REAL TRUE LOVE all about?"*

Well, as I have said, we found the answers to our questions.

We found our Christian faith in God and it was the solid rock that we needed when the storms came. Renée and I, each in our own way, weathered the on-rushing waves of despair and anguish and fear and heartbreak. We have been a little soggy, but never drowned, windblown, but not blown away, shaken, but not broken. We have grown stronger in the tempest.

Our faith in God, and our unconditional love for Jessica as a result, has been the eye in the center of the hurricane and our inspiration. Jessica's life intertwined with ours, and heated in the crucible of this unexpected tragedy, has forged us into something greater than any one of us could have been alone. It has been both a humbling, vibrant experience and a miraculous growing experience, embracing life with this little *'blessed one,'* because she has blessed us. We have been blessed way beyond my ability to adequately express it to you.

All I can do is try my best.

I have had my dark moments, but deep down inside, my faith in, and knowledge of, the truth of God, has revived me. Remember, I said I was a skeptic, but I was intellectually honest and I sought the answers. I attended lectures by Josh McDowell and James Dobson and many others. I read books and listened to tapes, and tried the *'evidence'* to the limit, and when the results were in, I knew the truth and so can you.

I have to agree with something, Josh McDowell, the former agnostic and skeptic, once said. *"Even though I have traveled the world in defense of Christianity and talked to many thousands of people, about the evidence for Christianity, I have only encountered a mere handful of people who had a 'genuine intellectual problem' with Christianity, most have a 'lifestyle' problem."* In other words, you have to be very honest with yourself. Do you really want to know the truth?

I promise you, if you really do want to know the truth, you can.

Why not be free?

If you have never honestly checked out the facts, I encourage you to do so. It could be the most important thing you have ever discovered. It was for me.

In the *'Appendix'* you will find a few suggested books with which to start. All you need is to be intellectually honest.

Who knows? Maybe you are almost at the top of the roller coaster, or just heading up? The downward rush is coming.

If you want to survive and grow stronger in your life's special situations, realize that you are not alone. God makes it very clear in the Bible that you have to choose to be alone.

I hope you will *'choose wisely.'* You will, won't you? If you do, He will never leave you, or forsake you.

A BIG personal question.

For obvious reasons, there is another area about which we often get questions. It is the *'vaccination'* question.

The overwhelming concern that parents of young children often have after they hear our story is, *"Should my child have the shots?"*

I debated addressing this question, but finally decided that I would be dishonest to avoid the issue. I do have opinions I must share. I agree that this is a very personal decision that every parent must make. So, for what it's worth, here is my *personal* answer. Remember I am not a doctor or a medical professional. I am the parent of a *vaccine injured child.*

Prevailing medical opinion says that vaccinations are not a bad thing, *but* you should be able to make an informed decision, because after all, who is signing the authorization forms and taking all of the responsibility? *It is you, not your doctor.*

My first suggestion is to ask your doctor about the dangers of all vaccinations. You will be asked to give your children many of these. DPT, measles and polio are common.

If your Doctor tells you there is no such thing as vaccine injury or talks down to you for being a panicky parent, (Sometimes well meaning medical people will say, "...*well you know... it's a numbers game...*") My advice, and it's what I did, is to find another doctor. If they have that opinion, they are either under informed or under educated or willing to risk *'your children'* because of their biases. Be very careful. You can't undo it.

I think you can understand the strong feelings I have, since I know first hand that vaccine injury is a very real threat.

Exercise caution.

Once again, I want to make something very clear here. I am giving you my personal opinion. I am not saying that you should avoid all vaccinations. I can explain my position best with this illustration.

I have seen airplanes fly and I have traveled on them. I know they are very safe and efficient and rarely malfunction or crash.

However, I don't think that as a result, we should stop spending the money and time on implementing and exercising airplane safety. Even heavily trained pilots do what is called a *'walk-around'* before taking off. They circle the airplane and check out things for themselves, before climbing in the cockpit.

It is the prudent thing to do. It is the smart thing to do.

When it comes to your child and your family, you are the *'pilot.'*

Be smart. Be prudent. Remember you cannot 'unring the bell.'

Here are a few other personal, practical guidelines based on my experiences and research over the years:

(1) There is a nervous system developmental process called 'myelination' that is important to understand.

When your baby is born, their nervous system is all in place, but not fully protected. Think of it as a bunch of wires without any insulation. During the first 18 months or so of their life, this 'insulation' grows over their 'bare wires,' so to speak.

Thus, the 'myelination' process. Until that is complete, their system is virtually unprotected from an attack on their nervous system and brain. It makes no sense to me to give them vaccinations when they are only months old and in that unprotected state. In addition, up until about two years old, they are still at an increased risk of damage *and* are unable to give you direct feedback. They can't tell you how they feel. Why risk it? Remember, you are in charge of your child. How safe do you want to be?

(2) If your child has been sick in anyway, *within six weeks* of the shot, wait. Their immune system may be weak or compromised. (especially true if they were premature) The schedules can be flexible. Exercise caution here. Your choice.

(3) I don't believe in clustering the shots (i.e. Diphtheria *and* Pertussis *and* Tetanus or DPT all at the same time) There is no medical reason for doing this... it is for *convenience* only. You can separate the shots, and in some cases use oral types as a substitute. I have seen *no studies* that check the safety of this 'clustering' practice. As far as I know they do not exist.

(4) Any history of reaction to vaccinations in your family?
If so, proceed with *extreme caution.* You are at a greater risk,
or at least in a higher risk group. Once again, remember you are
in charge of protecting your child and some things can not be
undone. Be an *educated* and *informed* parent.

I had never heard of severe injury from DPT shots until I
experienced it first hand. If you want my advice, don't be naive.
Remember, doctors are no different than plumbers. Get a good
one. *Don't be bullied or intimidated by any medical person.*
Vaccine injury is very real and very permanent.

The sad part about vaccines, is that the vaccine manufacturers
have turned the system into a *'profit center.'* Curing disease
and helping mankind takes a backseat to other ambitions.

In the USA we are the most vaccinated population in the world.
Yet many *odd afflictions* shadow the rapid growth in vaccine
production and administration. Check it out at *www.NVIC.org*

The *'Vaccine Injury Act of 1986'* was designed to address most
childhood vaccination injuries. (DPT, Polio and Measles)

If you think your child or a child you know has been injured in
any way by their immunization vaccinations, you should check it
out. I have included some information and websites for you, in
the *'Appendix.'*

Recent research indicates that my daughter was most likely
injured by the additives in her DPT vaccine. What I am
encouraging you to become, is a proactive parent. *Be aware of*
the perils so that you can protect your child as needed.

Love is another tool at your disposal, when trying to cope with the disabled and developmentally impaired or injured person. Handicapped children are just like the the rest of us, we all need love and acceptance, and lots of it.

I am not talking about the '*bat your eyes*' kind of love. I am talking about '*real*' love, true 'unselfish love' as described best in the Bible. You have to die to yourself and love others, without expecting anything in return.

'*Sacrificial love*' is the only love that will last.

Love the disabled unconditionally, and show it in your actions. They need to feel it in your voice, and in your touch. I was told by well meaning professionals that Jessica was just an empty shell and would never lead a productive life. They said that, "*She would be just as happy,*" locked up in what I would call, a cold gray institution, where all of her '*needs*' would be met.

Hmmm... I don't think so.

Probably one of the greatest things we have done for her was that we just loved her without reservation. We held her and we hugged her and we kissed her and tickled her feet. We showered her with affection, and at the same time treated her with dignity.

Love is never wasted. In fact, it is probably the most universal language in the world, reaching even those who can't speak.

We have loved Jessica unconditionally, and guess what? She loves us back. Our hearts are broken like humpty dumpty, but we go on, knowing that the day will come, when no more tears will be needed, but not just yet... no, not yet.

Jessica is now in her thirties. We are in our seventies.

It just seems like yesterday that she grabbed my finger so fiercely the first time we met. I marvel at how we have all grown up together... Renée and I and our other two children.

Our love has grown, our empathy and unselfish love for others and each other has grown. Our loyalty and concern for each other has grown. We have staggered forward, helping each other when have we stumbled, and we have grown stronger.

I would imagine that, some people look at our lives and observe, *"They have taken their broken child and tried to fix her as she grew up,"* but the truth is, Jessica fixed us, refining and improving us over the last 30 plus years, as we all grew up together. Jessica has changed us for the better.

What memories we have. God has been faithful to us.

The precious memories keep coming.

I remember when my grandson, Elijah James, was born. He was only a few days old when we went to visit him. As we were leaving we showed him to Jessica for the first time as she sat in her wheelchair. She looked him full in the face and broke into a marvelous dimpled smile. We all bawled like babies that day.

We have always kept Jessica in our family room in the middle of everything, where the action is, so she can be included, as much as possible, in everything that happens day to day.

When Elijah was three years old, I remember watching him tenderly trying to help Jessica up, when she fell while trying to sit up on her pad on the floor. Finally, succeeding in helping her, he looks at her with an approving smile and reaches over and tickles her ribs and goes, *"kootchie koo, Jessica."*

I had to turn away with tears in my eyes.

A few years ago, I made Jamie and Jon matching chess sets. They are identical and made from the same pieces of wood. I wanted to give them for sentimental reasons. Something that would always link them together over the years. Some of the cherry wood I used is from a huge cherry tree they used to play on, that once stood in our back yard. On the inside of the lid is the following inscription on a brass plaque:

> *"For I know the plans I have for you,"* declares the Lord,
> *"plans to prosper you and not to harm you,*
> *plans to give you hope and a future."*
>
> Jeremiah 29:11 NIV

That verse pretty much sums up our outlook for the future.

I know we will likely face more perilous times together, but everything will work together for good in our lives. For instance, in January 2004, we made another trip to the emergency room and Jessica spent another six days hospitalized. Not fun.

While she was in there however, she received respiratory therapy with a new device called 'The Vest®'. It is kind of an inflatable life jacket looking thing, that applies pressure and pulsing vibrations, to clear and keep clear her lungs and airways.

Seeing how effectively it worked, we decided to pro-actively give her twice daily treatments at home. Guess what? They had recently introduced a compact and completely portable unit.

We now have one, and it has improved Jessica's respiratory system, circulation and muscle tone. It is an amazing machine manufactured by an amazing company. See the *'Appendix'* for more information. So that gruesome hospital trip was a *'blessing in disguise,'* as they say.

There is one more Bible verse that comes to mind, if you will bear with me. It is another favorite of ours.

> *"For you created my inmost being; you knit me together in my mother's womb. I praise you because I am fearfully and wonderfully made; your works are wonderful, I know that full well.*
>
> *My frame was not hidden from you when I was made in the secret place.*
>
> *When I was woven together in the depths of the earth, your eyes saw my unformed body. All the days ordained for me were written in your book before one of them came to be."*
>
> Psalm 139:13-16 NIV

Your future and mine are coming under the watchful eye of God... ready or not. Kind of a sobering thought, I think.

I can see my future in my mind's eye.

Someday, I will walk out of a lovely forest into a sweet meadow of waving wildflowers. The air will smell fresh and fragrant and alive. I will look up into the rising sun and see a small figure walking towards me across the field.

Growing Up with JESSICA

As I watch, she will begin to run like the wind towards me. Throwing herself into my arms and hugging me fiercely, she will shout, *"I love you daddy!"* and I will answer with joy, *"I love you too, Jessica. I have always loved you."*

Then later... much later, I will reach out for her beautiful delicate hand, and we will go for a long walk among the singing forest of trees, because we will have a lot to talk about... and we will have all of the time we need.

That's my future... growing up with Jessica.

'Jessica... the Dreamer'

Epilogue: Ten years later...

It is now the summer of 2015 and Growing Up with Jessica has been in circulation over 10 years. Some things have changed and we have changed some of our viewpoints.

Our Family has Grown.

We celebrated our 50th anniversary! Our oldest Jamie was married in 2006 on my birthday, so I had a very nice birthday party! Our son Jon now has three little boys, as Benjamin David Walker came to join the tribe on January 18, 2007.

Our first grandaughter, Emerson Elizabeth Cilley came on board May 18, 2008. She spent the first week of her life in the critical care unit at the same hospital where Jessica was born. Her mom and dad gave her the same middle name as her Aunty Jessica. She is now fully recovered and doing fine.

Reactions to this Book.

When I first tearfully wrote *Growing Up with Jessica*, I said that if just one person was helped by the sharing of our journey through 'Jessica-land,' it would be worth the pain.

Overwhelming positive response has exceeded my hope by a thousand-fold. Meeting and talking to the many people who have been touched, inspired and lifted by reading our story has been a huge blessing and gives even more meaning to our lives.

Here is an example from a wonderful letter we have received.

"...I know I won't be able to find the proper words to describe how I felt while reading it and when I was finished. What best describes what I am thinking and feeling is the statement: 'My heart is full.' "

Thanks to all of you for your prayers and encouragement. Because of you, our 'hearts are full' as well!

The Vaccination Issue.

When you write a book like this you get many questions, and as I anticipated, many of them were about vaccinations. This caused me to do a lot of research on the subject, which I hadn't done a lot of since we solved our *'mystery.'* Doing research back then was *'stone age'* compared to the internet experience today.

There is a wealth of information out there. I have listed on page 198, three of the best sites for parents who want to make informed choices and protect their kids.

The research and study that I have done in the last ten years has changed some of my viewpoints on the vaccine issue.

The Awful Truth.

Firstly, the *Vaccine Injury Act of 1986.* Vaccine manufacturers use it as a shield to promote and propagate a whole slew of questionable vaccines, promiscuously and without any fear of legal repercussions for their dubious way of operating. This makes a mockery of the three stated objectives of the act.

The *'no fault'* compensation has become an adversarial contest, to discredit parents who file claims. The *'education'* and *'reporting'* functions are notoriously under utilized and misused, and the *'incentives for the production of safer vaccines'* is nonsense. In fact, vaccine makers, can throw caution to the winds since they are legally protected, as they profitably exploit the market.

We in the USA are the most over vaccinated population in the world, yet our children are plagued by mysterious afflictions and ailments. In my opinion, the *Center for Disease Control* (CDC) is in lock step with the vaccine manufacturers, not with the public that they are sworn to protect. It is a very sad state of affairs.

Please protect your children. Know the dangers and your rights!

The Appendix...

2002

...A Resource Guide.

Growing Up with JESSICA

Appendix

This Appendix includes a variety of information and resources in the hopes that some or all of it will help you or someone you know.

Contents:

Renée's Favorite Poem

Books, Resources & References

The Vaccine Injury Act Information

Therapy Equipment "The Vest®"

Photography Notes

Your Review Requested

Jessica's First Smile

Renée's Favorite Poem

Renée found this in a devotional book and we adapted it from the original by Edna Masimilla. We have personalized it for Jessica and it has been an encouragement to us over the years.

'Heaven's Very Special Child'

A meeting was held quite far from earth;
It was time again for another birth.

Said the angels to the Lord above.
"This special child will need much love.

Jessica may not run or laugh or play...
...her thoughts may seem quite far away.

In many ways she won't adapt,
and she'll be known as 'handicapped.'

So let's be careful where she's sent...
...we want her life to be content.

Please Lord, find the parents who will do...
...a very special job for you.

They will not realize right away...
...the leading role they are asked to play.

But, with this child sent from above...
Comes stronger faith and richer love.

And soon they'll know the privilege given,
in caring for their rare gift from heaven.

Their precious Jessica so meek and mild...
...is heaven's very special child."

Books by Josh McDowell:

Here are some of our favorites by Josh, updated. Interesting that we had included this list, long before Josh ever laid eyes on *'Growing Up with Jessica.'* Updated to include his latest.

'The NEW More Than a Carpenter'
ISBN 978-1-4143-2627-6 (180pp.)

NEW! In this revised and updated edition, former skeptic Josh McDowell is joined by his son, Sean, as they tackle the questions that today's generation continues to ask about Jesus.

Since its original publication, over 15 million copies of this book have been distributed in more than 85 languages and it continues to change countless lives. Now, this inspirational classic has been *updated* for a new generation of seekers, with a fresh look, revised material, a new chapter and now includes new content that addresses questions raised by today's popular atheist writers. Answers to questions like:

> *'Is this first century Hebrew carpenter truly the God he claimed to be?'*

> *'Or was he just a good man and maybe a little crazy?'*

This book offers arguments for faith from a skeptic turned believer. Read the story. Weigh the facts. Experience His love.

It provides a great overview of the issues and is very clear, concise and readable. It is easy to understand and yet presents a powerful, compelling case for the true identity of Jesus Christ.

"The NEW Evidence That Demands a Verdict"
ISBN 978-0-7852436-3-2 (760pp.)

Is the Bible historically reliable? Is there credible evidence of Christ's claim to be God? Can Christianity stand up before 21st century critics?

The New Evidence That Demands a Verdict is rated as one of the top 40 most important books of the last century. It is like an entire library in one volume and contains a tremendous amount of depth and breadth on the subject matter. Maintaining its classic defense of the faith, this fully updated volume provides historical, archaeological, and bibliographical evidences for the basic foundations of Christian belief.

This book continues to be one of the most comprehensive resource books on the evidence for Christianity, ever published.

In today's culture, where truth is relative and all religions are seen as equal, Christians face a growing challenge to know their faith is relevant and credible.

If you are a skeptic, or just want a strong basis for what you believe, then this book is for you.

Heartily recommended.

'GOD Breathed'

ISBN 978-1-63058-941-7 (216 pp.)

Join Josh as he provides clear evidence that God's Word is living, relevant, reliable and historically trustwothy. Sharing his own story as a *'skeptic turned believer,'* and his recently acquired, *'never seen before'* ancient scriptural artifacts.

Recapture the awe, the mystery, the passion and the power of Christian scripture.

Shiloh Run Press

About Josh McDowell Ministries:

Josh has been joined by his son Sean and together they have a tremendous resource of books, seminars, multi-media and free downloads to answer any questions in the following areas: *Is Jesus Really God? Can I trust the Bible? What is the Evidence for the Resurrection?* Questions about Sex and/or Relationships.

You will find their great website at **www.josh.org**

For a Complete Resource Catalog... of all of Josh & Sean's books and materials write to: Josh McDowell Ministries, P.O. Box 131000, Dallas, TX 75313. **Offices are located at:** 660 International Parkway, Ste 100, Richardson, TX 75313

Focus on the Family Ministries:

This is another excellent resource for your family. They also have an excellent 'Focus on the Family' newsletter which is free for the asking. They also have an E-newsletter.

Check on them at their great website: **www.family.org**
Focus on the Family, Colorado Springs, CO 80995

Books by Dr. James Dobson:

Raising our family we found these books to be very helpful. We recommend them to anyone who has kids. You will find them indispensable when it comes to family relationships.

'The NEW Dare to Discipline' ISBN 978-0-8423050-6-8 (276pp.)

As new generations of parents face the age-old challenge of helping children grow into responsible adults, many are turning to Dr. Dobson's classic parenting best seller. This instructive book reveals time-honored principles that are still relevant - even in the midst of today's shifting values. Raising our children, this is one the best and most practical books we have read and used.

'The NEW Hide or Seek' ISBN 978-0-8007568-0-2 (230pp.)

In this book, the founder of 'Focus on the Family,' offers 12 solid strategies for protecting kids from feelings of inadequacy and inferiority. The 'New Hide or Seek' best illuminates the needs of children, and addresses common concerns such as appearance, intelligence, shame, violence, acting out and others.

We found this book very critical in helping our children develop and be successful with their own unique gifts and talents. We highly recommend this book for raising confident, self assured and motivated children that grow up to be their own person.

Other Special Books by Dr. Dobson:

'The Mentally Retarded Child and His Family'
Access Available through the Educational Resources
Information Center(ERIC) on-line program.
www.eric.ed.gov:80/

This was the first reference book on the subject that I read.
I don't know if this book is still being published but you can at
least find it on-line at the above web site. You may very well find
it helpful reading if you are interacting with a retarded or
'handicapped child.' Great section on childhood seizures.

It is helpful in understanding both the mental ailments you may
face and their impact on your family. At a critical time in my life,
I found a great deal of comfort in Dr. Dobson's writing.

A Final Thought about 'Special Needs' children:

We like to think, that with Jessica we have been worthy of God's
trust. One thing we know for sure, He values her as a person of
worth and values her greatly. There is a verse I like to read, and
insert Jessica's name in it when I read it...

Then Jesus took a small child and had (her) stand among
them. Taking (Jessica) in his arms, he said,
"Whoever accepts a little child like (Jessica) in my name
accepts me. And whoever accepts me accepts the
One who sent me."

Mark 9:36-37 NCV (emphasis mine)

Who knows, perhaps the 'little child' who Jesus stood before
them was '...a very special child...' just maybe, a little girl who had
never 'stood' before? Imagine how sweet that would be.

The Books in the 'Growing Up with Jessica' Series:
Christian Choice Book Awards, DOUBLE Winner:

'First Place'
'Best Parenting Book'
and one of three
'Grand Prize'
Winners.

Growing Up with Jessica: A True Story
Blessed by the Unexpected Parenting
of a Special Needs Child.

Print: ISBN 978-0-9800641-0-0
eBook: ISBN 9780980064124
New Tenth Anniversary Edition for 2015

This award winning true story, told clearly and passionately by Jessica's father is moving as well as inspiring.

Shaken to the very roots of their faith, they found understanding and ultimate victory as they *'grew up'* as the unexpected caregivers for Jessica.

Tenth Anniversary Edition
for 2015 (Paperback 204 pages)

A very touching and inspiring adventure that is part mystery, part tragedy, and 100% inspirational. It will take you on an emotional roller coaster ride through tragedy, love, faith, hope and blessings. You will finally emerge, touched and inspired, with a *'full heart.'*

"I encourage you to read this book because it will touch you, minister to you and my hope is that you will conclude, as I did, that you will become a better person and parent as the result..."

Josh McDowell, Author & Speaker

Lessons from Jessica: Ultimate Caregiving.
A Longtime Caregiver's Inspirational Guide to Understanding and Ultimately Succeeding at Caregiving.

Print: ISBN: 978-1-944080-00-6 (196 pp)
eBook: ISBN: 9781944080013

From James Walker, the *Award Winning Author* and Jessica's Dad.

Walker recounts the lessons learned and truths revealed over nearly 40 years as a 24/7 caregiver. Practical time-tested principles found in this 'caregivers guide' does show clearly the path to ultimate success.

Written to raise awareness, understanding, and support for *'caregivers, their families, friends and observers.'* He shares how to breakthrough, highlighting successful concepts and the *'ultimate privilege'* of providing the life-giving care, for another human soul.

Explained are practical ways to acquire the commitment, endurance, and unselfish love needed to become what he describes as an *'ultimate caregiver.'* Other topics include, the importance of friendships, personal character development, confidence, the miracle of hope, understanding patience, finding blessings, amazing joy and faith, understanding helplessness, the worth of the human soul, and the privilege of caregiving, all of which adds up to the *'ultimate caregiving'* experience.

He also weaves into his narrative, insights from the lives of *Viktor Frankel, Mother Teresa, Albert Schweitzer, Ann Sullivan, Helen Keller, Josh McDowell & Jesus Christ,* along with his own practical life experiences. And also includes simple and practical ways to offer support and encouragement. Anyone reading Walker's book will be encouraged and inspired by his guide to *'ultimate caregiving.'*

The National Childhood Vaccine Injury Act of 1986

The following information and resources may prove helpful if you or someone you know thinks they have been injured by a required childhood vaccine.

The Act, which was established when signed into law by President Reagan on November 14, 1986, is a no fault compensation system for persons injured or killed through the administration of three groups of vaccines (or their component parts) normally administered to young children:

> *DPT(Diphtheria/pertussis/tetanus);*
> *MMR (Measles/Mumps/Rubella);*
> *and Polio (live or inactivated)*

This Act was enacted to ensure a continuing supply of the vaccines. The availability of these vaccines had been sharply curtailed by manufacturers because:

(1) Courts were expanding the grounds for recovery in product liability actions; and
(2) Insurance to cover their increased exposure was becoming unavailable or prohibitively expensive.[1]

1. *'The National Childhood Vaccine Injury Compensation Program' by Paul T. Baird, Special Master, United States Claims Court.*

The VACCINE INJURY Compensation Program

'The National Childhood Vaccine Injury Act of 1986' (PL-99-660) is a vaccine safety and compensation system which:
> (1) created a no-fault compensation alternative to suing vaccine manufacturers and providers on behalf of citizens injured or killed by vaccines;

(2) helps prevent future vaccine injuries through education and an adverse reaction reporting system; and
(3) creates incentives for the production of safer vaccines.

Compensation is divided into two parts:

(1) Injuries or deaths **prior to October 1, 1988** (no matter how long ago the injury occurred):

+ A citizen may choose to pursue a lawsuit unrestricted.
+ A citizen could have filed a claim in the compensation system by January 31, 1991
(2) Injuries or deaths occurring **after October 1, 1988:**

If the claim was not filed by 1/31/91, the statute of limitations has run out.

The National Vaccine Information Center (NVIC)

This is a non-profit and invaluable advocate for all vaccine information and safety. They are an excellent resource if you think you have a child that has been afflicted by required vaccinations or you need more information to help you intelligently and safely navigate the vaccine cartels.

The NVIC publication, *The Compensation System and How It Works,* is available from the *www.vaccineinjury.org* website for a small donation. The publication contains detailed information on the compensation system, how to file a claim, what to expect, how awards are paid and examples of final judgments.

If you suspect a vaccine has injured you or your child, order this publication. NVIC also has a directory of attorneys who handle vaccine injury claims.

Vaccine Adverse Events Reporting System (VAERS)

All suspected vaccine reactions should be reported to the *Vaccine Adverse Events Reporting System (VAERS)* operated by the Food and Drug Administration. Health care providers are *required by law* to report reactions. *If your doctor will not report any adverse vaccine reaction, NVIC will provide you with the forms so you can self report your reaction and or injury.*

Three Excellent Vaccine Information Web Sites:

www.nvic.org

This is one of the oldest and best sites around. They are very proactive in the area of vaccination safety and usage. Excellent.

www.novaccine.come

Site sponsored by *World Association for Vaccine Education (WAVE)* Want to know specifics about any vaccine? What is in the *'soup'* they are shooting into our kids? Answers found here.

www.vaccineinjury.org

Find out about the currrent status of the vaccine injury litigation process and current events at this site. This is the *Vaccine Injury Alliance*. Also has links to other important topics and resources. Will give you a *'leg up.'*

The Vest™ Airway Clearance System

We discovered this outstanding tool quite unwillingly when Jessica was hospitalized with a severe upper respiratory infection. Such events are a fact of life for someone with her severe seizure problems.

This *Airway Clearance System* has been a lifesaver. When we saw how well it worked on Jessica and the positive effect on her overall health, we knew we had to have one.

Millions of people in the United States besides Jessica, suffer from chronic respiratory conditions. Many of these people have a need for airway clearance therapy.

Here's how The Vest™ works.

The system consists of an inflatable vest attached by tubes to an air-pulse generator, which rapidly inflates and deflates the vest. This gently compresses and releases the chest wall very rapidly to create air flow within the lungs. This process mimics natural coughing and moves mucus toward the large airways where it can be cleared by further coughing or suctioning.

The technical name for this process is *'high frequency chest wall oscillation'* or... HFCWO. It sounds complicated but it isn't and believe me, it works! So if you have airway issues contact them.

The company is a very compassionate and amazing organization and I can't recommend them highly enough.

For more information see their website at:

www.thevest.com

Photography Notes & Credits & Comments

This is a listing of the photos shown. All are listed by description, date or approximate time frame, and photographer, if they were taken by someone other than a member of our family.

On the Cover. Jessica in her red dress. One of my favorites, a photo probably taken about age 9 in 1987.

How to Share Your Comments:

To share your comments and feedback with us please write to:

The Walker Family, Attn: Jessica's Dad, P.O. Box 8334, Boise, ID 83707 or e-mail: *jessicabookboise@gmail.com*